S0-DNJ-081

DATE LOANED

30 Jan '48Q

13 Feb '49 ER

7 Apr '50 M V
5 Sep '50 HS

26 Mar '55 R

28 Sep '56 V

11 Nov '57 CO

31 Oct '59 D C

12 Jan '61 B

22 Oct '61 A K

Control Desk

Control Desk

31 Oct '62 JG

29 Jan '6 K

EDUCATION and
World Tragedy

The Rushton Lectures

LONDON : GEOFFREY CUMBERLEGE

OXFORD UNIVERSITY PRESS

EDUCATION and World Tragedy

The Rushton Lectures

HOWARD MUMFORD JONES

HARVARD UNIVERSITY PRESS

Cambridge, Massachusetts

1946

COPYRIGHT, 1946

BY THE PRESIDENT AND FELLOWS OF HARVARD COLLEGE

PRINTED AT THE HARVARD UNIVERSITY PRINTING OFFICE

CAMBRIDGE, MASSACHUSETTS, U.S.A.

378.73
J
c/2

LA
226
J64

Kel 24Ja48

24 N 47 2.00 SUS (Adm.)

362478

FOR

Bessie

PREFACE

In the following pages I have tried to unite two qualities not easily fused together; whether I have been successful only the reader can judge. I have tried to be plain spoken about higher education and at the same time to be suggestive rather than dogmatic about educational programs, to write, in other words, for the next few years and the present parlous situation of Western culture rather than for time and eternity. The "ipse dixit" quality of much educational writing seems to me to generate more friction than warmth.

The reader will detect my indebtedness to half a dozen admirable pronouncements about education and the contemporary world — books by Wallace B. Donham, Eric Fischer, Elton Mayo, Alfred North Whitehead, F. S. C. Northrop, Quincy Wright and Erich Fromm, all of whom seem to have penetrated more deeply into the cultural dilemma of the twentieth century than have most of the formal reports on education.

I am grateful also to Walter Rideout, the faculty of Birmingham-Southern College, and to officials of the Carnegie Foundation and the Guggenheim Foundation for sympathetic counsel. But the chief source of strength in these pages has been my wife.

The statistics in chapter one are collected from various sources, often contradictory; later "authorities" may revise some of them. One difficulty is the word "casualties," which sometimes refers to killed and wounded, sometimes to killed, wounded, prisoners, and missing. But whether the eventual totals shall prove smaller or larger than mine is irrelevant. The picture remains appalling.

The substance of these chapters was delivered on the Rushton Foundation in Birmingham, Alabama, in April, 1946, as a series of three lectures. This admirable enterprise, which it was my privilege to inaugurate, is dedicated to civic education. Another, smaller portion of the book formed the substance of a commencement address at Hofstra College in June, 1946.

HOWARD MUMFORD JONES

Peacham, Vermont
August 1946

CONTENTS

EDUCATION AND WORLD TRAGEDY

EDUCATION AND WORLD TRAGEDY

If any human being brought up in the tradition of western civilization could, by some miracle, step outside the familiar patterns of that culture; if history could come to him with the same shock of surprise that a new and stimulating novel brings him; if, in sum, retaining the moral idealism of western civilization as a standard of measurement, he could yet discover for the first time what has happened to mankind in the last fifty years, such a person would, I think, be overwhelmed by a single tragic conviction; namely, that the history of mankind for the last half century has been a history of deepening horror.

Since 1896 the earth has scarcely known a year without warfare, armed revolt, massacre, pogrom or other ingenious form of slaughter. During the first thirty years of the present century, according to Quincy Wright's authoritative study of war, European powers alone fought seventy-four wars, which lasted a total of 297 years; roughly, the average war was four years long. One has to go back to the twelfth century to find a comparable record. In that unenlightened century the average war lasted only three years and a half.

These fifty years include two infernal conflicts — World War I and World War II. They include such disastrous struggles as the Boer War of 1899–1902, the Russo-Japanese War of 1904–05, the two bloody Balkan Wars of 1912–13, the innumerable wars, revolts, "interventions," and massacres in Finland, the Caucasus, the Ukraine, Poland, Hungary, Manchuria, Siberia, and other "border" areas, which followed the Bolshevik Revolution of 1917. They include the long drawn out agony of China, which, beginning with the massacre of garrison troops in 1917, continues to this hour. They include the intermittent civil war in Spain. These are the major events.

But there were other episodes, tragic in their time. Who now vividly remembers the Formosa rebellion of 1896? The Cretan massacre of 1897, when Christians slaughtered the Moslem peasantry? The Boxer rebellion of 1900? The Philippine insurrection and the "water cure"? The massacre of a million Armenians between 1896 and 1919? Yet all these are soberly chronicled in any encyclopedia.

The year 1922 is as representative as any. The Irish civil war was raging, and there were Black and Tan outrages. The year opened with the slaughter of 300 Greek civilians in Samsun. By August about 100,000 Greeks had been killed or captured (I do not know the figures for the Turkish dead), some tens of thousands of civilians having been slain. The bloody climax of 1922 was reached at the taking of Smyrna, when an estimated 200,000 Christians were rendered homeless and the city was given over to pillage, rapine, massacre and fire.

Even at the risk of monotony one must chronicle other wars in this unhappy half century. There was an earlier Graeco-Turkish war in 1897–98, and an Italo-Turkish war in 1911. Between 1928 and 1935 Bolivia and Paraguay fought to exhaustion over the possession of a tropical jungle. Indeed, during many, if not most, of these fifty years there have been rebellions in Latin America; and though it is sometimes said that armed revolt is the standard form of presidential election in that distressed area, a man dead of a bullet in Caracas or Asunción will no more come to life again than a man dead of a bullet at Vimy Ridge or Bataan.

The half century has seen armed rebellion sweep through such famous capitals as Paris, Berlin, Madrid, Athens, and Rome. It has seen more or less protracted revolutionary struggles in Russia, Mexico, Spain, France, Germany, India, Egypt, Palestine, the other Arabian states, Mongolia, China, Hungary, Austria, Greece, Iran, and various other countries, besides what uncounted minor uprisings — Nicaragua, Haiti, Albania, Thailand and the like — only the *World Almanac* now tells us. Ours is a sick age.

How many human beings have been killed directly

or indirectly in the course of this terrible history? It is almost impossible to find out. One man's guess is as good as another's. Statistics about death by warfare are not kept in some continents, and, moreover, by its very nature modern warfare sometimes destroys both record and statistician. For example, we do not know and probably shall never know how many hundreds of thousands have died of violence in Asia and Africa during these fifty years. How many perished during the obscure struggle for the control of Tannu-Tuwa, a country twice as large as Scotland, lying between Mongolia and Siberia? How many Koreans were slaughtered by their Japanese overlords? How many natives died during the struggle for the control of the Belgium Congo? We do not know, just as we do not know how many hundreds of thousands died in Russia, on its borders, or in neighboring states during the terrible convulsions that swept over the future Soviet Union between 1914 and the adoption of the constitution of 1925. We do not know how many millions Hitler and his agents killed. But what we know with rough accuracy is sufficiently appalling.

Before 1900 about 25 per cent of all battle casualties died; in World War I this increased to 33 1/3 per cent. In the seventeenth century it is estimated that, out of every thousand Frenchmen, 11 died in military service; in the twentieth century, up to World War II, 63 thus perished, an increase of al-

most 600 per cent. Out of every thousand Europeans
alive in the twelfth century it is thought that two
died as battle casualties; in the first twenty-five years
of the twentieth century 54 out of every thousand so
died, an increase of 1700 per cent. Professor Pitirim
Sorokin estimates that during the first third of this
century Europe suffered 24 million war casualties. If
we slaughtered or wounded every man, woman, and
child in Maine, New Hampshire, Vermont, Massachusetts, Rhode Island, Connecticut, New York, and
New Jersey tomorrow, we should about equal this
number.

From the eleventh to the twentieth centuries war
casualties totaled about 18 million. In the first three
decades of the present century we have therefore
killed 33 1/3 per cent more human beings than were
killed in the previous 800 years. But these figures do
not include five other continents, and they take us
only to the rise of Hitler. There were, it is thought,
ten million dead in World War I. Influenza, typhus,
starvation, and other destroying agencies killed some
ten million more. But these figures are principally for
Europe; the best guess for the whole world is that 40
million died, directly or indirectly, in World War I.
To equal this number of Americans we shall have to
add to the slaughter of New England, New York,
and New Jersey, the deaths of every man, woman and
child in Pennsylvania, Delaware, Maryland, and the

District of Columbia — a little less than one-third of the total population of the United States.

We do not yet know the figures for World War II or for the conflicts that preceded it like the civil war in Spain, which, however, accounted for about two and one-half million dead. One tiny state — Luxembourg — lost 4000 in battle and at least 500 others executed by the conquerors. Twenty-five thousand civilians alone were killed in Belgium. The dead in Holland were at least 200,000 (this does not include later deaths by malnutrition). In Yugoslavia during the resistance to the Germans in 1942–43 there were one million dead; a million more were killed from 1943 to 1945. The Japanese dead are reckoned at more than three million. About three and one-half million Poles were shot, murdered, gassed, starved or tortured to death. According to a correspondent writing in *The Christian Science Monitor* for November, 1945, from Poznan to Stettin the Polish plain, once a granary for Germany, is for 150 miles as "barren and neglected as a desert" and cannot support a new population for indefinite months.

The German dead up to the summer of 1945 are estimated at eight and one-half million; how many have since died of starvation or of vengeance is unknown. The military dead in China from 1937 to 1944 are nearly three million; the civilian dead anything you like — ten million, twelve million, twenty million. One figure for Russian losses gives 21 million casualties of all sorts. A United Press dispatch from the Vatican in November, 1945, estimated the dead, military and civilian, in World War II at over 22 million, the wounded at 34 and one-half million, or 56 million casualties in all. The population of the entire South, including Delaware and Maryland, in 1940 was 41 millions. If every man, woman, and child in Alabama were butchered they would number less than half the number of Jews butchered in Europe since 1933. If the entire population of the United States were wiped out tomorrow, their number would be less than the number of human beings who have died of violence, disease or starvation in war or as a result of it during the last half century. It doesn't make sense.

While this blind struggle continues, it increases its ferocity. Through the mouth of Satan in *The Mysterious Stranger* Mark Twain sardonically remarks, "No brute ever does a cruel thing — that is the monopoly of those with the Moral Sense." I turn to the formal indictment listing the criminal acts of the Nazis for illustrations of the Moral Sense of mankind. This document includes only those crimes for which there is legal evidence. Here is a summary of one sub-section of one indictment only — the subsection covering murders and tortures in eastern Germany and western Russia.

The figures run: at Maidanek 1,500,000 persons exterminated; at Auschwitz, 4,000,000; in Lwow and its environs, 700,000; in the Livenitz forest and environs, 133,000 Jews tortured and shot; in Ganov, 200,000 peaceful citizens exterminated by "the most refined methods of cruelty," mass shootings taking place to the accompaniment of orchestral music furnished by players who were next to be shot; in the Ozarichi region, tens of thousands interned, many dying of typhus injections; in Esthonia, on one day only, at Camp Klooga, 2,000 persons shot; in Lithuania, at Paneriai, at least 100,000 killed; in Kaunas, more than 70,000; in Alytus, about 60,000; at Prenai, about 3,000; at Ukmerge, about 8,000; in Mariampole, about 7,000; in Trakai and its environs, about 37,640; in Latvia, 577,000 murdered; at Smolensk, 135,000; near Leningrad, about 172,000; in Stravopol, tens of thousands; in Pyatigorsk, an unknown number; in Krasnodar, 6,700; at Stalingrad, 50,000; in Orel, 5,000; in Novgorod, many thousands; near Kiev, 100,000; in and about Rovno, one million. There is another column of particulars for this part of Europe alone.

Here is one of the more bearable paragraphs describing the manner of these deaths: "After the Germans were expelled from Stalingrad more than 1000 mutilated bodies of local inhabitants were found with marks of torture. One hundred and thirty-nine women had their arms painfully bent backward and held by wires. From some, their breasts had been cut off and their ears, fingers, and toes had been amputated. The bodies bore the marks of burns. On the bodies of the men the five-pointed star was burned with an iron or cut with a knife. Some were disemboweled." The full bill of particulars may be read in *The New York Times* for October 19, 1945.

These dead are at peace. Unnumbered thousands of human beings live on in a world-wide condition of famine. Unnumbered thousands of human beings whose lives have been wrecked by war or starvation or despair or disease still exist. Regarding the long-range results of war upon our lives Professor Wright tells us:

Closely related to the racial [i.e., human] cost of war but . . . less susceptible to objective measurement are the social and cultural costs of war in the deterioration of standards. Wars of large magnitude have been followed by anti-intellectual movements in art, literature and philosophy; by waves of crime, sexual license, suicide, venereal disease, delinquent youth; by class, racial and religious intolerance, persecution, refugees, social and political revolution; by abandonment of orderly processes for settling disputes and changing law; and by a decline in respect for international law and treaties.[1]

The standards of only a few, he says, are elevated by war, a minor gain which by contrast deepens the gloom of the general picture.

---

[1] Quincy Wright, *A Study of War*, 2 vols. (University of Chicago Press, 1942), I, 246.

"Deterioration of standards" is a vague phrase. Three sets of parallel instances may make vivid what Professor Wright has in mind. In 1903 Americans were horrified to learn of an anti-Jewish pogrom in the city of Kiev. Strong denunciations of Russia were uttered by church groups and others. In this pogrom 47 Jews were killed and 700 houses destroyed — altogether an amateur affair. Yet in 1945, although the Germans are known to have massacred between six and seven million Jews by means extending from simple shooting to "the most refined methods of cruelty," foreign correspondents reported that many American soldiers were finding the Germans the most agreeable Europeans they had met and deciding that the horrors of the concentration camps were either incidental or the invention of propagandists.

Again: in 1937 Vittorio Mussolini, warring against the blameless Ethiopians, was roundly scolded by sensitive Americans for saying: "To me war is a sport — the most glorious sport in existence. . . . I remember that one group of horsemen gave me the impression of a budding rose as the bombs fell in their midst." One supposes that if a hundred horsemen were killed as petals of the budding rose, the bomb was singularly successful. Five or six years later, American airmen were regularly cheered for their sporting prowess in bringing down Japanese planes; and the science reporter of *The New York Times* was thought in 1945 to have written a singularly effective prose masterpiece about the rare beauty of the atomic bomb upheaval over Hiroshima. This killed or mutilated, we are told, 140,000 or 150,000 human beings, 30,000 so completely that no trace of them remains.

The official report of the United States Strategic Bombing Survey as printed in *The New York Times* Sunday, June 30, 1946, says that the mortality rate per square mile destroyed at Hiroshima was 15,000 and at Nagasaki, 20,000, and after discussing death by "flash burns" ("radiant heat of incredible temperatures that struck its victims with the speed of light") remarks that other victims were bombarded with visible and invisible rays:

> The victims of these rays who did not die instantly were made sterile; pregnant women suffered miscarriages; some lost their hair, suffered diseases of the mouth, pharynx and intestinal tract, or they had hemorrhages of gums, nose and skin.
>
> There is reason to believe that if the effects of blast and fire had been entirely absent from the bombing, the number of deaths among people within a radius of one-half mile . . . would have been almost as great as the actual figures and the deaths among those within one mile would have been slightly less.
>
> The principal difference would have been in the time of the deaths. Instead of being killed outright . . . they would have survived for a few days or even three or four weeks, only to die eventually of radiation disease.

It is encouraging to read that at distances between 6,500 and 10,000 feet from "zero point" of the bomb, one-third of the pregnant women gave birth to apparently normal children.

A third and final example: in 1917 one-tenth of the city of Halifax was destroyed by the accidental explosion of 3,000 tons of TNT. Immediately cities like Boston rushed food and supplies to the devastated area, asking no question about the politics of the sufferers or of the administrators of the relief work. In 1945, when the lives of millions, some of them our allies in World War II, almost literally depended upon our ability to move food into devastated Europe, the Congress of the United States haggled for months over the politics of the administrators, refusing to appropriate necessary money though hundreds of thousand starved. Such are the coarsening effects upon our finer sensibilities of an uninterrupted diet of blood.

II

It would of course be possible to add other illustrative examples. One of our chief reasons for entering World War I was that we were morally outraged by unrestricted submarine warfare; in World War II we delighted to wage successful unrestricted submarine warfare ourselves. In 1937 the destruction of men, women and children in the city of Guernica by aerial bombardment during the Spanish civil war seemed to many liberals morally outrageous. In 1945 American aviators blasted Nagasaki off the map, killing civilian men, women and children by the thousands, but there was no effective protest. So deep have we descended into the pit that Dr. Irving Langmuir, Nobel Prize winner, physical chemist and associate director of the General Electric Research Laboratories, solemnly warned a joint meeting of the American Philosophical Society and the National Academy of Sciences in the autumn of 1945 in Philadelphia that so-called atomic warfare, unless the release of nuclear energy is controlled by the world, may make the entire earth uninhabitable, wiping out the ignoble race of men. Dr. Langmuir is a conservative scientist. He spoke sadly and seriously. The Americans read his words in such of our irresponsible newspapers as bothered to publish them and then turned to the sports pages. We do not believe things like this because we do not wish to believe them.

Dr. Langmuir's statement suggests a second basic fact in this brutal history. It is that modern warfare is increasingly a function of education, and education is increasingly dominated by war. We do not like to think that this is so. We try desperately to deceive ourselves. One form of optimistic rationalization is the "progress" fallacy. The progress fallacy assumes that mankind always survives any conceivable weapon.

Thus, precisely as the bow and arrow rendered the

club ineffective, so the invention of gunpowder made the bow and arrow obsolete. Precisely as the airplane made horsemen useless, so the atomic bomb has rendered existing weapons obsolete. But as mankind survived these earlier shifts to deadlier modes of destruction, so mankind will survive Dr. Langmuir's threat of planetary suicide. Therefore, although the problem is serious, the terms of the problem of atomic energy are the same terms as those of the bow and arrow problem. We need not worry, or at least not worry too much. The argument of course ignores the mounting tide of unnecessary destruction, the loss of potential human energy, and the setbacks to genuine development along our historic road.

Let us examine this logic. Doubtless the first club bearer wounded by a distant bowman marvelled at the new technology before he died. Ere long, however, his tribe had been trained to manufacture bows and arrows. So, too, after gunpowder superseded bows and arrows, both sides eventually manufactured gunpowder. But there was a significant difference. Fewer men in any society can manufacture rifles than can make bows and arrows, because the manufacture of rifles depends upon the possession by a minority of the population of technological skills, proper factories, power, and sufficient raw materials. To insure the existence of these things requires a higher concentration of educational facilities than is required in the bow and arrow society. And of course a still smaller number of persons can make or use the highly complex artillery of yesterday's warfare than can make or use rifles and shotguns, and only a few scientists and technologists and only a few industrial societies can turn out atomic bombs. Therefore it is that the increasing intricacy of our lethal weapons is a function of the increasing technological skills of the human race. This of course means that in modern civilizations a constantly decreasing percentage of the population is directly capable of creating the weapons of modern warfare, so that some H. G. Wells of the future, taking a leaf from Aristophanes, may show how a future war was stopped by a sit-down strike of scientists, technicians, and skilled laborers.

Of course our technological skills are not used solely for warfare, but in view of the increasing length, ferocity, and destruction of modern war this is not now the point, especially since, in time of war, technological skill devoted to destruction has the highest possible priority. Certain it is, moreover, that the latest destroyers of humanity — the torpedo, the submarine, the airplane, the tank, poison gas, the rocket, and the A-bomb — are products of highly educated, or at least highly trained, personnel. All but one or two of these are principally or wholly the products of American technological ingenuity. We missed out on poison gas, but we made it up on the atom bomb.

However, the connection between warfare and education goes deeper than the simple but impressive connection between destruction and technical training. The training of soldiers, sailors and airmen grows increasingly complex. If Hitler and Mussolini were men of no particularized education, their rise to military power was abnormal rather than typical, and for the most part, in modern times, the men who launch wars and who manage them are products of professional education at least as exhaustive and specialized as the education of a doctor, a physicist or a lawyer. Members of a modern general staff devote their lives to study, so that a traditional military leader like General Forrest or Mad Anthony Wayne would not know what to make of these studious and intellectual careers.

Indeed, during World War I, William Jennings Bryan was quaintly out of date when he said that in case of invasion the American people would spring to arms — something that the technological advance of the nineteenth century rendered ineffective and impossible. Nowadays it is impossible for a nation to spring to arms in the old-fashioned sense; and if minute men leaving the plow for the musket sufficed for Lexington and Concord, not even the Home Guard would have sufficed for the Battle of Britain if the German invasion had come. The *lévee en masse* of the French Revolution is antiquated in a world in which the elementary education of a private or of a common sailor takes three months, and a year is considered essential for lasting training — a year filled with educational exercises of such rigor that the colleges cannot compete in intensity. If anarchy should settle over the globe, it is of course possible that a new and illiterate Attila or Genghis Khan might raise, equip and lead popular armies, but in the contemporary world warfare like industry depends primarily upon the continuation and advance of highly complex engineering and scientific studies.

This dependence comes by and by to affect not merely the training of the fighting man, it affects in time the life of the civilian. The difference between a war fought by the professional army of Frederick the Great and total warfare in the twentieth century is that the entire population participates in modern warfare, not merely in the sense that it may reasonably expect to get killed or wounded, but also in the sense that it shares to greater or less degree this professional training, even if it is no more than civilian street patrolling, the care of children in deep underground shelters, or assignment to an "essential" factory. One has to look back at the relative indifference of most of the population in the American Revolution, the War of 1812, or the Mexican War to see how

far we have come. Even during the Civil War life in
the North went on as usual, and civilian energies were
so little controlled by warfare that the settlement of
the West went forward, mining was developed, and
shipping, agriculture, and industry increased, partly,
to be sure, as a function of warfare, but mainly in a
normal mode of progression which the war stimulated
but which the fighting did not bend to its own purpose.
Contrast the control of civilian life by Washington
in World War II. Contrast the even more rigid control of national existence in the British Isles during
the same period and since.

Education, then, becomes more and more involved
with warfare as warfare develops. Use and wont have
of course accustomed us to this strange alliance between destruction and education. Looking backward,
we can see how far we have advanced along our fatal
road. When in 1808 Napoleon created the University
of France as a single body to direct education in his
empire, he may have intended to conscript men's
minds as he conscripted their bodies, but the ministry
of war did not take over the University of Paris, invade its classrooms or establish a special military curriculum. On the contrary, even under despotism, the
University of Paris operated as a civilian institution.
So, too, when Frederick William III founded the University of Berlin in 1810, that institution, though it
was meant to be "a weapon of war as well as a nursery

of learning," made its martial contribution in the field of the spirit only. Its curriculum was not dictated by Prussian generals, and *Lehrfreiheit* and *Lernfreiheit*, two essentially civilian concepts, were from the beginning the theoretical principles of its life. In the same epoch Britain sometimes stood alone and sometimes feared an invasion from the Continent. Yet Oxford, Cambridge, St. Andrews, Edinburgh and Dublin universities pursued the peaceful tenor of their civilian ways.

In the United States neither the War of 1812 nor the war with Mexico touched the life of our colleges significantly. During the American Civil War Northern colleges and universities, though diminished in manpower, continued to function; and Professor Theodore W. Hunt of Princeton, who lived through that period, tells us that "during the four years of war" there was "no general or protracted suspension of college work, no such nervous tension existing as that which we have noticed in these tragic days of international strife." (He is talking about World War I.) In the South, of course, colleges ceased to exist where the students enlisted or where the buildings were destroyed, but these institutions were never taken over by the Confederate War Department as institutions. Even so recent a conflict as the Spanish-American War left the American universities to themselves.

The American Civil War nevertheless had a profound effect upon our collegiate education. It is true that in the light of modern science and technology, that war was fought on lines as primitive as the wars of Xerxes. But in 1862 the Morrill Act extended federal aid to individual states which would agree to create technological and agricultural colleges. This act sprang from the growing conviction that the superior potential of the nation in transportation and industry must be preserved. The effects of this act, adopted during a period of war, have been epochal. In 1860 there were four engineering schools in the country; in 1929 there were 148 technical colleges. In 31 years ending in 1866 only 300 engineering degrees had been granted; by 1917 these degrees numbered 60,000, and the number of engineering graduates per million of our population had increased from 3 to 43. Among the institutions owing much to the Morrill Act are the Massachusetts Institute of Technology and Cornell University. The law requires each college profiting by it to institute courses in military training or to offer equivalent instruction.

In 1916 the National Defense Act further enriched the alliance between war and education by creating in the colleges the Reserve Officers' Training Corps, which was for a brief period eclipsed by the Students' Army Training Corps, established in October, 1918, in more than 400 colleges and enrolling 140,000 men.

The significant fact is not the success or failure of this short-lived enterprise, the significant fact is that the colleges accepted it almost without protest, as part of their duty to the nation. Drs. Capen and W. C. John averred that the Students' Army Training Corps "saved colleges from virtual extinction" in World War I. But the War Department Committee on Education and Special Training had earlier declared that the "sole purpose . . . repeatedly stated by the War Department was to increase the military power of the country." In other words, education was made subordinate. President Thwing of Western Reserve University, in his history of higher education in World War I, flatly states that "the colleges became, like the railroads, essentially government institutions," that "students pursued a course of study which was either military or colored by military conditions," that "academic standards were arbitrarily set aside; academic methods were condemned; military standards, manners, and methods were installed" and that "in the development of the Students' Army Training Corps the Federal Government approached more nearly than by any other method or measure to the German procedure of the control of higher education." To Dean Boyd of the University of Kentucky, writing in 1919, it seemed a happy thing that "our educational system" was "still virile enough to make of itself a special tool for a special purpose." But of course an educational system thus virile, when it becomes a special tool for a special purpose — in this case, technological preparation for destruction — ceases to exist except as a special tool. And albeit the colleges were returned to civilian aims, the fact had been discovered that they could be quickly converted to war.

However, the creation of soldiers, particularly of a skilled officer personnel, was not the only task of higher education in World War I. The present American Council on Education grew out of a movement organized in January, 1918, to "place the resources of the educational institutions of our country more completely at the disposal of the National Government." That one of the highest purposes of an educational institution operating on *Lernfreiheit* and *Lehrfreiheit* might be to avoid commitment to governmental policies was something the statement ignored. War research under the National Research Council then, as later, occupied the attention of academic research workers, to the exclusion of pure science. Commitment to governmental policies was more important in technological warfare than commitment to the increase of knowledge. The change was defended as necessary to national existence. The defense, if it be one, illumines the history of the increasing alliance between education and war.

Of the six aims set up by the National Research

Council two were avowedly military: "the quicken-
ing of research in the sciences and in their application
to the useful arts, in order to increase knowledge, *to
strengthen national defense*, and to contribute in
other ways to the public welfare" was one; and "to
call the attention of scientific and technical investigators *to the importance of military and industrial
problems in connection with the war*, and to the fur-
thering of the solution of these problems by specific
researches" was the other. (My italics). All this was
doubtless necessary, but if the processes of history
are necessary, we cannot avoid facing the implications of historical determinism. If scientists have
been lately perturbed by the threat of governmental
control of research, the various bills in Congress designed to safeguard the secrets of nuclear energy for
military purposes or to subsidize scientists as a means
of strengthening the national defense are simply the
logical carrying out of the aims of the National Research Council established by the Academy of Sciences in 1916.

In World War I half the college laboratories were
working on war problems under conditions which had
nothing to do with the search after knowledge for its
own sake. Training was characteristically military.
Replying to a questionnaire, the Case School of Ap-
plied Science could say that "all courses are taught
more or less with war in view." The *Princeton*

Alumni Weekly declared in 1917 that "every day Princeton becomes less an academic college and more a school of war." Another educational historian, Dr. Kolbe, describes World War I as "in a broad sense a college man's war," says that the "colleges practically forced their services on the Nation," and remarks that "a period of war . . . made of us a military nation and has militarized our system of higher education."

At the conclusion of hostilities war-time controls were taken off the colleges, which reverted to their civilian status. The explanation is sometimes therefore advanced that the conscription of the colleges for military purposes is a highly abnormal procedure, which must not be mistaken for national policy. The defense does not defend. Having discovered in World War I how useful the colleges could be, the nation in World War II converted them to adjuncts of its military system much more quickly and efficiently because it had the experience of World War I to go on. World War II, in sum, simply broadened and extended the relation between war and education worked out some thirty years ago, and our experience is so recent and familiar as to require no exposition here. So gradually does one become accustomed to imperceptible change that it surprised nobody to find the laboratories of great universities surrounded by armed guards and inaccessible even to officers of the institutions which owned them. One further step in the story must, however, be noted. If World War I put college men into uniform, World War II turned women's colleges into military and naval establishments, and one beheld without any amazement an institution like Smith College become a training ground for the WAVES and young women in uniform marched by platoons to classes in the Harvard Business School.

III

A final fact to be observed in this strange, eventful history is to note how nationalism increasingly invades education. The eighteenth century was perhaps the last period when a truly international culture was the common object of study, at least among cultivated classes in the western world. But the schools of the eighteenth century were still characteristically under the control of the church, of princes who prided themselves on participating in the Enlightenment, or of private persons and corporations. As yet education was not customarily created or paid for by the state.

Throughout the nineteenth century, however, and increasingly in the twentieth, the doctrine that education is a proper charge against the public purse has meant that the state, in greater and greater degree, has made education the instrument of its own support. Thus a leading element in the Chinese Revolution was the demand for state-supported schools, schools that would in fact teach doctrines acceptable to Dr. Sun Yat Sen or, latterly, doctrines acceptable to the ministry of education of Generalissimo Chiang Kai-Shek. Thus the Bolshevik revolution destroyed every vestige of Czarist or Greek Orthodox schools and created a system of education which is as much an arm of the state as the Russian air force or the Russian infantry. Even in a small and unmilitaristic country like Norway, government has in fact forced the abolition of private schools. In Italy, in Germany, in Japan, in Spain, the educational system has been integrated with the state to such a degree that in taking over conquered countries the Allies had to begin by abolishing the remnants of existing schools, destroying textbooks and substituting new systems of education that would mirror and support their own political doctrine. And in France it is a nice question whether the church or the state shall control the schools. Again, in a self-conscious state like Eire one finds government through the schools forcing Gaelic, a cumbersome and artificial language, upon the people as essential to a "national" culture.

Nor is the New World exempt from this nationalism. In Latin American countries political revolution so frequently starts in the universities that successful dictators — Cuban history will furnish examples —

either close down these institutions or control the faculties and the students by repression, censorship, "coördination" or exile. The struggle in Mexico for the control of education has been one of the spectacular elements of the cultural history of that nation in the twentieth century. The unhappiness of "liberal" Argentine intellectuals is increased under the Peròn regime by government determination that education shall support the state in return for state support of education.

For Thomas Jefferson it was sufficient that teachers should possess rationality and virtue; he did not envision the teachers' oath law now common among the states of the American Union. The compulsory flag salute, almost universal in American schools, is a twentieth century invention. *The New York Times* launches a campaign to make American history compulsory in high school or in college. State legislatures pass laws forbidding state-supported institutions to employ those who are not American citizens.

Even at advanced levels it is usually difficult and sometimes impossible for experts to examine in American classrooms theories of the state, of politics or of economic development held to be "un-American," as witness the recent tempest about courses in Russian civilization at Cornell. An American historian writes a whole book in answer to the question: Are American teachers free? and accumulates innumerable instances to show that they are not free to contradict or question national prejudices and policies, even though the teacher is convinced these are wrong.

Negatively, this perfervid nationalism is part of the xenophobia of an age in which instruments of communication have prematurely thrown cultures into collision with each other before the peoples were ready to understand one another. Positively, this nationalism, which has rallied religion, culture, technology and science itself to its support, now includes education — it is a necessary part of something called "national defense." The idea would, however, have been completely incomprehensible in the medieval university.

In connection with this nationalism the admirable "Report of the United States Education Mission to Japan" submitted to General MacArthur at Tokyo on March 30, 1946, is interesting and illuminating. This document is the product of a committee of 27 American educators called to Japan to advise the commanding general about the Japanese educational system. Again and again the report recurs to the excessive nationalism of schools in that island empire before defeat. The committee felt that the "purging of vicious elements" in the teaching profession was well along and that "the spirit of national Shintoism and military aggression" was being eradicated from the schools by "straightforward directives." It felt that educational reform must deny "ultra-national-ism." As the first step in any conceivable reform, it approved "the discontinuance, in the public schools, of partisan teaching, political or religious," and recommended the ending of centralized control of textbooks, teachers, and schools, the stopping of ceremonies that have served "the purposes of a militant nationalism" and the abolition of "Thought Control." It suggests many wise improvements. It urges that a revamped Ministry of Education should be given "veto powers concerning militaristic or ultra-nationalistic activities in the schools, such powers to be explicitly stated in the law and limited." This is certainly admirable, and one does not see, in the limited time at the disposal of the Mission, how its recommendations could have been improved.

But if a thoughtful Japanese were to inquire whether any official body in the United States possesses "veto powers concerning militaristic or ultra-nationalistic activities in the schools," limited or not, the answer would have to be no. Moreover, the Mission found itself in an insoluble dilemma. On the one hand, it wanted to abolish "ultra-nationalism" because ultra-nationalism had become a menace to the world. On the other hand, it could not abolish Japanese tradition, history, or culture. Negatively, it knew what it wanted. Positively, it took refuge in phrases like these:

It should be the task of all engaged in the educational activities of Japan to analyze their cultural traditions in order to discover what is worth preserving as humane ideas and ideals that will give strength to the new plans. Here the Japanese will find a legitimate and inspiring basis for loyalty and patriotism.

. . . . freedom of teaching and of inquiry must be encouraged not only for the preservation but for the enrichment of the national culture of Japan.

Boys and girls alike should . . . grow up knowing their national constitution, for it is the institution under which majority rule prevails.

[Children] must be prepared to take the lead. The future of Japan rests upon their shoulders.

One has every admiration for this report, perhaps one of the most remarkable educational documents of the twentieth century. But at what point are the children, upon whose shoulders rests the future of Japan, to check their loyalty and patriotism? Suppose a majority of the Japanese under the constitution decide to reinstitute the system the Allies have just abolished? Suppose that, in their study of ways and means for the preservation and enrichment of the national culture of Japan, the Japanese decide that the Allied attempt to abolish Shintoism was a misguided venture, motivated by Occidental capitalism and cunningly designed to reduce Japan forever to the inferior status of a vassal nation? Is perfervid nationalism right in the United States and wrong in Japan? If the majority of Americans vote for flag salutes, why should the majority of Japanese be prevented from voting for a ceremonial bow in the direction of the imperial palace? If the fortunes of war had reversed themselves, would the Americans be satisfied with an "inspiring basis for loyalty and patriotism" strictly limited to Oriental notions of international comity and the exchange of teachers?

All this is said, not in disparagement of the commission, but because the report innocently throws a flood of light upon the interconnections of nationalism and education in the modern world. Our problem is the ancient problem: *Quis custodiet custodes?* When even the international comity of scientists is disrupted by an iron curtain across Europe, governmental controls of investigations into nuclear energy, passport difficulties, military interference, and the discharge of investigators, however brilliant, who are not of the right political faith, the concept of learning as an a-nationalistic body of knowledge common to educated men everywhere has suffered some severe practical limitations. In the field of the social scientists, it is commonplace, the judgments of an expert in Moscow and one at the University of Texas, for example, about the defects and merits of free capitalistic enterprise will scarcely coincide. The cautious suggestion of the Japanese educational mission that Japan had better begin thinking about birth control was so worded as to avoid a quarrel with the Vatican, and the sociology permitted in the Turkey of Must-

apha Kemal was, one suspects, not quite on all fours
with the sociology taught in Brazil. As for the humanities, literary censorship in Eire seems to ban
books for study that are commonplace in London or
Oxford; Mr. Walter Lippmann complained that there
is now no common tradition of philosophy, literature
and the arts to which, amid the jarring nationalisms
of our time, western men can rally; and the approach
in Mediterranean countries to the study of the classics differs *toto caelo* from that in the United States.

War, technology in preparation for war, and nationalism — these are, then, three great forces warping
the healthy development of education in what we
quaintly call the civilized world. The problems they
raise are deeper and darker than those polite fictions
discussed in most educational meetings, especially at
the college level. In truth, one sometimes fears that
our concern for the nature of education, notably at
higher levels, seldom rises above the plane of the
genteel tradition. Certain it is, however, that an uneasy sense of something wrong, of some radical error,
haunts our schools and colleges, troubles philosophers, and leads even the common man to endless
speculation about the future of his own civilization.
The sense that western culture is wildly astray, western civilization in its decline, is everywhere about us
as men turn once again to examine the fundamentals

of what they believe. If this chapter is gloomy, one cannot alter it. We can only ask, so far as the subject of this book is concerned, what educators themselves have to say on these, the terrible problems of our time.

Face to face with the spectre of war, with technology controlled by war, and with an intense and irrational nationalism which, as in the case of the atom bomb, dreams of going to war before some other nation shall invent an even more terrible weapon — and this, in a world in which the nations have solemnly pledged themselves to unite for peace — what have American schoolmen to offer for the guiding of mankind? There is no more tremendous question before the United States.

For, as Dr. Raymond B. Fosdick said on almost the last day of the victorious year of 1945,

No greater crisis was ever faced by any generation in history. Our enemies are not Alaric and his Goths pouring over the frontiers of the north. The enemies that threaten us are of our own creation; they are the techniques which we have ourselves perfected and which we have allowed to be perverted to unworthy ends. How do we bring these techniques under social control? How do we keep them from making a mockery of all we have hoped or dreamed of good? That is the challenge of the present crisis; those are the insistent questions that are hurled at our generation; and whether or not the future is to be a nightmare without end depends upon our ability to make some headway in finding the answers.

What does educational theory propose? And if, as may be the case, the proposals of educational theory shall prove not altogether satisfactory, how shall we set about finding more satisfactory answers to the problem of education and world tragedy?

DOCTORS DISAGREE

DOCTORS DISAGREE

American optimism being what it is, the preceding discussion of the relation between war and education may well seem one-sided, morbid or gloomy. There are of course elements in our civilization brighter and better than those we have just analyzed. For example, throughout the past half-century medicine has prospered, great foundations have sent their benefits over the earth, and a variety of international organizations from Rotary International to the Rockefeller Foundation have done their share to improve the lot of man. Science and technology are not and have not been instruments of destruction only; on the contrary, they may yet turn out to be the means of our salvation. New instruments of communication offer at least the hope of a more rational intercourse among nations. Business itself, charged in the nineteen-twenties with being merchants of death, knows now, if it did not know then, that wars destroy customers, profits, investments, raw materials, credits, currencies and, finally, even business. Moreover, international controls and the weight of opinion even in these dark decades have occasionally prevented, localized or ended armed conflict. In any

extended history of our time we should have to estimate events and forces which, if they have not
stopped, at least have slowed our descent into the
abyss. And it is of course the hope of man that the
United Nations will succeed in ending the threat of
a third World War, which, should it occur, will almost
infallibly destroy western civilization.

Although objective history would speak of these
matters, it is still true that the curve of human hope
has steadily descended for fifty years. Moreover, the
developments of the last twelve months in the United
States alone are not conducive to optimism. Political
observers tell us that neither Congress nor the president leads a nation in which pressure groups spring-
ing from our technological culture exert more influence
upon legislation than does the concept of either one
nation or one world. The general intent of business,
small and large, seems to have been to throw off war-
time controls and to revert to the idea of a free market, despite the obvious fact that a free market does
not and cannot exist in a world of wrecked currencies,
starvation, destruction and social chaos. Hope for
genuine intercultural understanding between Russia
and the nations of the West grows more and more dim
as old-line statesmen resume the futile game of power
politics. "Communism" is denounced as anti-Chris-
tian by the largest Christian body in the country, despite the fact that the issue of our time is not whether

communism is a form of heresy, but whether mankind shall survive to be either orthodox or heretical. The military hospitals are filled with human wreckage, yet irresponsible officials are happily planning another world war. The United States is the leading technological nation in the world. It was instrumental in setting up the United Nations as a device for securing permanent peace to mankind — and yet, twelve months after the ending of hostilities in Japan, it maintained the largest army in its history, kept a navy larger than all the other navies of the world put together, demanded bases in the Atlantic and the Pacific far beyond its boundaries — and was then surprised and vexed to discover that other nations, such as Russia and Great Britain, are suspicious of its motives. It is not the philanthropy of UNRRA (checked by a distrust of Russia, as it is), but the creation by technology and science of the atomic bomb that is central to the next ten or fifteen years. Witness Bikini.

Our problem is then deeper, more radical, and alas! more nearly insoluble than a simple balancing of general gains in health, longevity, good will, and control of nature against the stupendous losses of war, and if one speaks of the "next ten or fifteen years" as crucial, it is only because the direction taken by western man in this period will probably determine his existence or disappearance within a century. And that these are not the alarmist views of a mere literary man (and therefore of an abnormally sensitive and, by inference, morbid person) is shown by the sober statements of students of our business civilization. One of the profoundest analyses of this culture, a book which has stolen on the world without the notice it should have had, is Professor Elton Mayo's *The Social Problems of an Industrial Civilization*. A member of the Department of Industrial Research of the Graduate School of Business Administration at Harvard University, Professor Mayo cannot be called a radical. But after twenty years of studying industrial relations in the United States, he writes:

> Technical skill manifests itself as a capacity to manipulate things in the service of human purposes. Social skill shows itself as a capacity to receive communications from others, and to respond to the attitudes and ideas of others in such fashion as to promote congenial participation in a common task. . . . In these days, education has gone over — often extravagantly — to the development of technical skills and the appropriate scientific bases for such skills. This would be excellent were it not for the fact that the universities have failed to develop an equivalent study of, and instruction in, social skill. . . . *We have in fact passed beyond that stage of human organization in which effective communication and collaboration were secured by established routines of relationship*.[1]

Again:

> We have undertaken to transform an economy of scarcity into an economy of abundance, and the technicians are showing us the way. We are committed to the development of a

[1] Division of Research, Graduate School of Business Administration, Harvard University, 1945, p. 13.

high human adaptability that has not characterized any known human society in the past, and it is our present failure in this respect that finds reflection in the social chaos which is destroying civilized society.[2]

And again:

Under the influence of economic theory, we have a system of education that trains young men in technical understanding and technical skill; we do nothing whatever to develop social insight or to impart social skill. Indeed we provide an education that operates to hinder the development of such skills. And the general public, business leaders, and politicians are left with the implication that mankind is an unorganized rabble upon which order must be imposed. It was this delusion that encouraged Hitler's dreams of grandeur.[3]

Finally:

We have failed to train students in the study of social situations; we have thought that first-class technical training was sufficient in a modern and mechanical age. As a consequent we are technically competent as no other age in history has been; and we combine this with utter social incompetence. This defect of education and administration has of recent years become a menace to the whole future of civilization.[4]

It is not only the opinion of Professor Mayo, it is the opinion of other distinguished students of culture — for example, Professor F. S. C. Northrop in his exhaustive and important volume, *The Meeting of East and West* — that our civilization must re-educate itself or perish.

But how re-educate? Re-education is a vast, vague word. The re-education of man, if it is to take place, is something to which formal schooling can contribute

[2] Mayo, p. 15.   [3] Mayo, p. 50.   [4] Mayo, p. 120.

only its minor share. Religion, science, the arts, custom, technology, industry, business, government, amusement — these and other human institutions pour out their multitudinous influences that are more important than formal education. For, despite all our fine talk about "training for leadership" in American colleges, we do not train for leadership,[5] our schools mainly reflect the interests of dominant groups in our society, they do not direct these interests. They are, in other words, what schools usually are, instruments of social conservation rather than dynamos of social change.

But though it would be folly to expect that some reshaping of our schools would immediately alter the course of history, it would be even greater folly not to demand of the schools such light and leading as they can give. It will be noticed that Professor Mayo's comments upon our social crisis are also comments upon the education of those who have brought the social crisis into being. That the schools are expected to do more than preserve cultural heritages is evident, as we have seen, by the central place which education occupies in programs for rehabilitating the nations from Norway to Italy and from Mexico to China. The creation in the United Nations pattern of

[5] The challenge flung down by Wallace B. Donham to the liberal arts college in his *Education for Responsible Living* seems to have been genially ignored as the colleges went peacefully back to "true and tried" educational ideals after V-J day.

UNESCO — the United Nations Educational, Scientific and Cultural Organization — is a crowning example of world-wide interest in the inter-relations between war, technological training for war and nationalism on the one hand, and education on the other.

Education is, then a world-wide problem. But in order that our inquiry may have immediate meaning, I propose to ask what suggestions are placed before thoughtful Americans for so re-shaping education as to avoid the errors of the past; and since even this is an enormous subject, let us limit the inquiry to higher education in the United States. The common schools have, with some justice, accused the colleges of being ignorant or indifferent to their problems, but I believe it will be possible for present purposes to avoid the collegiate parochialism implied in this criticism.

The catastrophes of the last half century have affected all parts of the American educational system. Nevertheless, it is roughly true that primary education has not been violently altered. Despite enormous increases in the high school population during this period, a re-orientation of the aims of secondary education, and profound changes in the high schools brought about by the depression, the draft, the shifting tax structure and other social forces, it seems likewise to be true that secondary education, though it has altered much more than has primary education, changes reluctantly and passively — indeed, the complaint of educational reformers is that this is so. But higher education is in many ways more directly affected by world events. It is an area more highly sensitized to industrial and political changes. Since in the long run it supplies most of the teachers and administrators for the rest of the school system, higher education permits us to inquire what theories are current and what alterations are contemplated at that level, the inference being that these theories and alterations ultimately affect even the kindergarten. The assumption is therefore a fair one that higher education today determines, in a general way, the nature of primary and secondary education tomorrow. It is not the sole determinant, of course, but it is a determinant of such force and comprehensiveness that with us higher education seldom points one way only to find popular education going off in the opposite direction.

What, then is the current trend of thought in the American college? What do leading academic educators propose? What do they suggest for the university world by way of leadership? What is their program for the democratic state a year or so after Hiroshima?

There is an enormous library, there is a vast body of experience to draw on. We have had pronouncements by Chancellor Hutchins and by a committee of the Harvard faculty; we have had publications by the University of North Carolina and by the educational editor of *The New York Times;* we have had reports from Columbia and Yale and we have had individual books and articles by writers like Mark Van Doren, the late Wendell Willkie and the living Walter Lippman; we have had special curricula like the one at St. John's College and we have had special schools like the General College of the University of Minnesota. We have also innumerable articles, essays, addresses and reports in the educational journals and out of them. And we have had the comments of the man in the street.

When we examine this material two inferences are immediately evident. The first is that, although there is very general agreement as to what is wrong with higher education, there is no agreement as to how to remedy its defects. The second is that these reports, these books, articles and addresses tend to come, not from all parts of the academic community, but from particular portions of it. It will be convenient to discuss the meanings of these two inferences in reverse order.

The proposals for change do not characteristically spring from the scientific parts of the faculties. This does not mean that scientists have not been appointed to some of the committees making reports, or that scientists are satisfied with educational processes or that scientists are oblivious to civic need. Indeed, to those naive persons (and there are a great many such, in the churches and out of them) who regard a scientist as at heart a materialist devoid alike of social responsibility and of ethical scruple, one can point out that the first protest against the use of our knowledge of nuclear physics for purposes of wholesale slaughter came from the scientists, none of whom was consulted about the bombing of Hiroshima; and that investigators of the rank of Dr. Urey, Dr. Rabi, Dr. Langmuir, Dr. Oppenheimer and others have selflessly devoted themselves to educating the rest of us into some sense of the dangers we confront. The notion that the scientist is professionally incapable of value judgments is one of the quaintest and most ignorant assumptions that so-called humanists can make.

Nevertheless it is generally true that, as a professional group, scientists have clung to the assumption that their primary academic business is research and the training of others to become research workers. They have not characteristically concerned themselves with academic administration except as academic administration has concerned itself with *them*;[6] and they have left to what a sardonic colleague calls the "talking departments" the formulation of educa-

[6] This does not mean that scientists have not served as deans, presidents, or other sorts of academic administrators in numbers proportionate to their academic strength.

tional theory. The consequence is that the library of books and articles on higher education has principally been the product of non-scientific members of the faculty, and oftener the work of the humanists than of the social scientists. The fact is of immense significance.

In a scientific and technological age our educational theory should not be shaped mainly by non-scientists. What is equally important is that whereas able scientists make some effort to understand the social scientists and the humanists, the humanists make little effort to comprehend the scientists, so that, when the humanists attempt to discuss science in the curriculum, they tend to talk about it as if they were living in the late nineteenth century wherein a simple, mechanistic theory sufficed. The effect of this error has been unfortunate. It has meant that, despite all these well intended efforts to restore unity to higher education, the two great halves of that education — the sciences and the arts, including social science — are being driven apart, as can be seen, for example, at the University of Chicago, where development in the natural sciences has gone forward with almost no reference to the struggle over neo-scholasticism and its Aristotelian postulates, that has convulsed other portions of the university.

But the relative absence of scientists from speculation about educational reform has not prevented an indirect but powerful influence from science upon schemes of academic education. The scientist is not to blame because humanists and social scientists, envying him surety of technique and mathematical modes of statement, have inevitably tended to believe that their own "disciplines" approach perfection in proportion as they become "scientific" — that is to say, in proportion as they can be subjected to technical and even technological manipulation. Economists, political scientists and sociologists are haunted by the ghosts of "scientific laws" in fields where human behavior is frequently strange and unpredictable; literary and philosophical research is supposed to improve in proportion as it achieves the impersonality, objectivity, and mathematical rigor of chemistry, nuclear physics or topology. "Research" in these fields is therefore innocently thought of as paralleling research in "science," and higher education in these fields, whatever formal deference it may pay to philosophic or civic ends, is perpetually veering in the direction of the perfect "research worker." However imperfect the scientist may be to himself, to other academic men he seems to walk with surety, to measure with accuracy, and to predict with skill; consequently humanists cannot, even when they want to, avoid stopping educational change precisely at that point where educational change is most needed. Undergraduate curriculums are subject to manipulation; but the training of those who are to teach undergraduates — that is, the graduate students of today who become the professors of tomorrow — remains unaltered. The scientific specialist claims the right to create scientific specialists. For him the undergraduate problem is minor. Consequently, in the effort to keep up the pace, humanists and social scientists, however great their concern for the undergraduate curriculum, imitate the scientist and retain the right to control the specialized education of their own graduate students.

II

The second element common to discussions of academic reform in the United States is general agreement as to the weaknesses that are found in college and university. Troubled because the colleges are unable to stem the forces of war, to restrict our vast technological preoccupation or to pass beyond nationalism; troubled, too, by a variety of other weaknesses such as vocationalism and shallowness, educational writers inquire why there is no united front in education and find there is no front to unite. They commonly charge that any concept of a general, liberal or common education has disappeared in the anarchy of the elective system, the particularism of the departmental organization of college faculties, and the pressures of vocational necessity. They say that educated men today speak no common language; that the liberal colleges give no common stock of ideas because they are vague in their aim, their professors being by nature and nurture incompetent to offer general training that is both broad and deep. They find in higher education no common concept of knowledge for its own sake; no agreement that a well-rounded character can be molded by such and such studies, and no governing ideal of lofty civic virtue. Some critics further allege that many colleges and universities are under political, religious and financial pressures of such character as to prevent them from fulfilling their real educational purpose.

Such is the indictment which, in varying forms, one will find in Mr. Flexner's study of American and European universities, in Professor Foerster's volume on the American state university, in Thorstein Veblen's *Higher Learning in America*, in Mr. Upton Sinclair's *The Goose Step*, in Chancellor Hutchins's book, *No Friendly Voice*, and in other books and essays by him, and in the pronouncements of Mr. Walter Lippmann. Reformers therefore set themselves the task of re-establishing a lost unity in higher studies, but as they do not agree on the nature of this unity, discussion grows acrid. I believe, however, that one can distinguish two general schools of thought as to the unity desired. The one group purposes to seek a dogmatic unity; the other wants to find unity in something called tradition.

At the extreme right among the dogmatists is the group of Roman Catholic colleges, with the great Catholic University of America at their head. In 1939 this institution, celebrating its semi-centennial, published a series of lectures entitled *Vital Problems of Catholic Education in the United States*. The first of these, by the Rev. Geoffrey O'Connell, is an unequivocal statement of the Roman Catholic position. "A new civilization and culture," says Father O'Connell, "are being molded in America, even as the civilization and cultures of the older nations in Europe decay. Catholicism in the divine economy must pollenize, permeate, and direct this vast enterprise, and one of its chief agencies must be sound education with principles and goals founded on abiding truth." [7] Abiding truth is found in divine revelation delivered to the infallible church. With philosophy theology is therefore the core of right education. "Since truth cannot contradict truth, and the false alone is opposed to the true, the philosopher realizes that if he arrives at a conclusion incompatible with revelation, such a conclusion must be false. . . ." Education has as its principal aim the assisting of man's spiritual nature to battle against his corrupt nature. It must

[7] "Catholic Education and Non-Catholic Philosophies," *Vital Problems of Catholic Education in the United States* (Washington, D. C.: Catholic University of America Press, 1939), pp. 1–21.

assist his natural reason until his human nature has "become supernatural." "The totality of Christian truths and ideals . . . founded on infallible dogma, inspires, permeates, and complements a complete philosophy of life underlying Catholic education." Outside the church American education springs from and is permeated by a spirit of "naturalism," "which uses the method and spirit of empirical science to explain everything in the universe." This naturalism it is the express aim of Catholic education to combat and overcome. There can be no compromise. And the reverend father concludes by saying that "Christian education has never really been tried outside of the Catholic educational system."

That the aim of Catholic education is lofty cannot be denied. Nor can it be denied that during long centuries of western history the church carried education in its bosom, a fact for which western man must be forever grateful. Moreover, Professor F. S. C. Northrop points out that the scholastic philosophy, to which Catholic orthodoxy is committed, was in its day a working scientific hypothesis, to which the church adapted theology after the rediscovery of Aristotle in the Middle Ages. But neither the lofty aim nor the historical facts answer adequately the query: is Roman Catholic educational theory the proper core for higher studies in these United States?

Three observations immediately suggest them-

selves and must be courteously urged. As Father
O'Connell candidly states, between secular education and "true," that is, Catholic education, there
can be no compromise. But since this church, though
powerful, is still a minority in a country that has
expressly adopted secular education as a public responsibility, it does not seem likely Americans not
of Catholic faith will agree that the only proper study
of Shakespeare and conic sections is one conditioned
by infallible dogma. In the next place, the majority
of scientists are by no means convinced that Aristotelian and Thomistic theory is the only (and proper) hypothesis for scientific advance; and in a society conditioned by technology, the wide adoption
of the Catholic theory must eventually depend upon
the acceptance by scientists of neo-scholastic postulates. But inasmuch as, according to Father O'Connell, the spirit of "naturalism" is eternally wrong,
even though the method and spirit of empirical science have been pragmatically successful in American
society, Catholic theory is face to face with an extremely stubborn historical fact.

Finally, Father O'Connell speaks of the decay of
cultures in the older nations of Europe. Some of
these decaying countries — for example, Italy and
Spain — are Catholic countries, in which education
is either under the control of the church or has been
(until recently) so long controlled by it as to have

tested the Catholic ideal in action; and though I am far from saying the Catholic church is any more responsible for the backwardness of education in Catholic countries than are the Protestant churches for the weaknesses of American education, which they once controlled, the general educational record of the Italy of Mussolini and the Spain of General Franco seems to indicate either a failure to implement the ideal of education urged or a refusal to grapple adequately with the problems of contemporary society. It is at least possible that Catholic education suffers from defects like those of the secular schools and is perhaps no wiser than the rest of us.

One turns to the second group of dogmatists with real misgivings because they complain that their point of view is not fairly represented except in their own writings, and also because, being skillful dialecticians, they respond to criticism by a flood of sophistic logic. I refer of course to the Chicago school of thought, which has its outlying colonies like St. John's College and its eastern proponents like Mr. Mark Van Doren, who, though he is not precisely a neo-Thomist, advocates prescriptive readings which come from St. John's. The twin pillars of this doctrine are, first, a return to the theory of the medieval university; and second, faith in a prescribed reading list. In its simplest form the argument runs that since the primary business of education is with the moral and intellectual "virtues," the proper organization of a college will be around the seven liberal arts of medieval fame — grammar, rhetoric, logic; and arithmetic, music, geometry and astronomy. The best mode of education will be dialectical — that is, after the manner of Aristotelian logic as reshaped by the schoolmen. The best aim of education is, in Chancellor Hutchins's phrase, that "moral, intellectual, and spiritual reformation for which the world waits." This seems to mean a return to authoritarianism, a kind of Catholicism without Christianity.

The second great pillar of the theory is that there is a small library of books of permanent value. These, in Mr. Van Doren's phrase, should be planted "at the center of the college curriculum," a proposal so simple "that it can be stated in one breath." Until this is everywhere done, he says, "we shall lack the right to say that liberal education exists among us." As some of the proponents of this reform prefer the authority of Plato to that of Aristotle and Aquinas, there is some difference in the degree of neo-scholasticism admitted, but in general this school believes wisdom and virtue are so overwhelmingly the products of past time that only by a return upon the authoritative sayings of a few masters can mankind be saved. They are therefore in general violently opposed to empiricism, "liberalism" and that most characteristic of American philosophies, the pragmatism of William

James. For them liberal education is expressly forbidden to have anything directly to do with learning to make a living; and though liberal education is theoretically open to anyone who can profit by it, in fact only a minority are practically found worthy of the liberal arts.

The great virtues of this theory, at least at Chicago, are simplicity and thoroughness. Albeit the application of the seven arts to modern knowledge (or rather the fitting of modern knowledge into the scheme of the seven liberal arts) becomes so strained as to lose all meaning, outside of the sciences (with which the neo-scholastics, most of them not being professional scientists, do not tamper), the followers of this theory have certainly reduced the confusion of the modern curriculum to an intellectual harmony, at least at the introductory stage, and this may, indeed, be valuable. Whether it is the right harmony, whether the resulting simplicity may not be too dearly bought one may doubt.

Believers in this system have also succeeded in securing from students, or at least from students persuaded of the truth of the theory, a degree of thoroughness of study hitherto principally associated with the sciences and the professions. This, too, is a good. But there has been also a concomitant repelling of other types of students quite as intelligent, yet not primarily dialecticians. And of course the weakness of dialectic is contentiousness, a fault that neither student nor professor has avoided. It is also unfortunate, though advocates of this view will not admit it, that in tracing human error to empiricism, these educators have in fact widened the split between modern science, experimental in method, and the teaching of the arts. Experimental science may, indeed, have helped to get us into our tragic state, but we cannot weaken, abolish or ignore it by a return to Aristotle, Aquinas or Plato. Finally, one may reasonably question whether an education authoritarian in tone can be widely imposed upon a victorious democratic society organized as a technological culture of great complexity and richness.

The second great pillar of this reform, it will be recalled, is the idea that there are about one hundred books — the actual number listed is more than 110 — the reading of which should be required of all educated persons. These books fall into two categories: classics of science, and other classics. In an effort to understand the history of science it is alleged that St. John's College students are also expected to repeat the experiments by which a Galilei or a Faraday made his discoveries. That a general grasp of scientific postulates is desirable in our society cannot be denied. That a method so cumbersome and inefficient as the historical repetition of experiments which have long since outlived their first usefulness is the only way or the best way to secure this end is an astonishing assumption.

The majority of the 110 titles are philosophical and literary and form a strange library, in which William James jostles St. Bonaventura, fiction is represented by *Tom Jones*, Voltaire, *War and Peace* and Dostoevski's *The Possessed*, and the contribution of the United States to the wisdom of the world is reduced to three titles. Only five of these books have any direct affirmative connection with the modern democratic state in which St. John's College exists and, except for Rousseau's *Social Contract*, not one of these five stands up squarely and fairly for the common man. The list, however, includes Plato, an apologist for the authoritarian state, Aquinas, an apologist for an authoritarian church, and Hobbes, an apologist for an authoritarian monarchy. It includes sceptics like Lucian, Montaigne, Swift and Hume; it includes Pascal, who taught that man knows nothing and can know nothing by the unaided reason; it contains Malthus, Darwin and Marx, who held that life is a ruthless struggle; it contains Hegel, the theoretical ancestor of Nazi Germany. You will not find in it the names of Thomas Jefferson, Ralph Waldo Emerson, Abraham Lincoln, Walt Whitman or Mark Twain, whom I cite, not because they are Americans, but because they are believers in the common man.

Inasmuch as the principal argument for this library is that it represents a tradition common to western man, one is puzzled to know what the tradition is or why it is appropriate to the modern democratic state. If the list approaches unity, that unity must lie in the majority of its titles, and the majority of its titles seems to indicate that the intellectual tradition of western Europe is, to a surprising degree, a tradition of scepticism, authoritarianism and despair of ordinary humanity. It is difficult to see how such a tradition can help education. If the list does not represent unity, I do not see that it really cures the confusion of the present curriculum. For, if these texts are to be intensively studied in order to develop some sort of coherent whole, confusion is increased by the necessity of finding a common denominator between Lucian, the Greek sceptic, and St. Bonaventura, the medieval Catholic; between Sophocles, who held that man is a noble being, and Swift, who held that he is not; between Rousseau, who trusted in altruism, and Malthus, who trusted in selfishness.

It is idle for believers in the list to retort to this criticism that to demand unity of doctrine from their library is to confuse teaching with indoctrination, for the reason that the very proponents of the list set it up as doctrine. Philosophical harmony, however, this library does not possess except as any hundred intelligent books have the harmony of intelligence.

But inasmuch as this harmony of intelligence is what the current course offering also claims — indeed, this harmony of intelligence is virtually its sole claim to unity — it is difficult to see how the St. John's College list advances education. One hundred disparate books, even though each one is an historic milestone, do not differ radically from twenty ordinary courses, each of which is devoted to an important aspect of culture. The unity of the list is neither formal nor real.

Nevertheless, the list is supposed to be the core of a liberal education, which is something distinct from "servile" education — that is, education directed towards earning one's living. Educators so uncertain of their idealism that they must first look it up in a carefully chosen library to see whether they have the sanction of a dead master, represent that failure of nerve of which the genteel tradition has been accused. A garage mechanic, confident of his tools, doing the best possible repair job, working cleanly and accurately within the pattern of his craft, would seem to be a far better, a more integrated citizen, even for Plato's commonwealth and Aquinas's university, than apologists for a liberal education thus remote from kindliness and actuality.

In fact, Mr. Dooley is still pertinent: "Readin', my friend, is talked about by all readin' people as though it was th' on'y thing that makes a man betther thin his neighbors. But th' truth is that readin' is th' next thing this side iv goin' to bed f'r restin' the mind. . . . Believe me, Hinnissy, readin' is not thinkin'."

III

We come now to those who wish in education to return to what they call tradition. The tradition to which they wish to return is something called the unity of western culture. In practical terms this has usually meant the creation of large general courses for undergraduates, courses which cross departmental boundaries, which are usually offered in the first two years of college, usually required of most students, usually taught by a special staff, their substance usually found in the social sciences and the arts. In addition, however, there have been attempts at the more difficult task of clarifying for non-scientists the assumptions, the issues and the working of science.

The historical course often takes form as "The Development of Western Institutions," "Sources of Contemporary Civilization" or something of like kind. Courses in the arts and philosophy tend to be of the Great Books, Great Thinkers or Great Masterpieces order, albeit a "general" course in philosophy is sometimes devoted to persistent problems, philosophical issues and the like. The general intent of the program is four-fold. It seeks to provide for all, not merely for undergraduates specializing in a single department (philosophy, English, history) a common core of training in the primary assumptions of western culture. It is intended usefully to restrict the anarchy of the elective system. It is meant to replace the present departmentalized introductory courses with something broader and more enriching. And it is supposed to renew student faith in our democratic society.

Courses of this order have been widely introduced, so widely, indeed, that a future educational historian may characterize the post-war epoch as one in which the nation turned defensively to reconsider the basis of its civilization. The popularity of this formula arises from the fact that it is flexible, from the truth that teaching such courses is less of a wrench to professors trained in their several specialties than teaching courses differing radically from standard instruction would be, from the opportunity for fruitful experimentation, and, above all, from the desire of students for philosophical guidance less dogmatic than authoritarian systems but nevertheless clear, simple and applicable to American problems.

Upon this revival of western traditionalism four several observations should be brought to bear. The first is the statement of William James that no priesthood ever originates its own reforms. As this reform originates within the priesthood, the problem is to determine whether it is reform or merely change. The second is the statement by Dean Carmichael of the University of Illinois in 1938 that, though there has been a great deal of writing and speaking about "modifying educational processes and adjusting them to current needs," "this has generally ended in discussion, and very little has been done in the way of effective action." We are, he said, still carrying on "the processes of education on essentially the same basis as that on which our predecessors dealt with them, notwithstanding the fact that the social process into which graduates of our institutions will go has undergone a marked change." Dean Carmichael's observation is generally in line with that of Professor Elton Mayo's *Social Problems of an Industrial Civilization.*

The third observation is the finding of Gerald Johnson that the common man doesn't care two straws about the humanities for the sufficient reason that the humanists have never learned to communicate with the common man. Perhaps the most glaring instance of this truth is the attitude of academic humanists to those who are concerned about the common schools, in which the children of the common man are mainly educated. Whatever their defects, members of the faculties of departments and schools of education and of teacher-training colleges are struggling with the vastest educational problem before the nation; they get neither sympathy nor understanding from academic humanists as a group.

The fourth comment is a profound observation, one of the profoundest observations of our time, made by a man whom many regard as the greatest thinker in the English speaking world. Professor Alfred North Whitehead wrote in 1933:

> Our sociological theories, our political philosophy, our practical maxims of business, our political economy, and our doctrines of education are derived from an unbroken tradition of great thinkers and of practical examples, from the age of Plato. . . . to the end of the last century. The whole of this tradition is warped by the vicious assumption that each generation will substantially live amid the conditions governing the lives of its fathers and will transmit those conditions to mould with equal force the lives of its children. *We are living in the first period of human history for which this assumption is false.* (My italics).[8]

Adventures in Ideas, in which this statement appears, was published the year Hitler came into power. The post-atomic-bomb world merely heightens one's respect for Professor Whitehead's power of divination. Unfortunately advocates of a return to traditionalism seem to have read only those parts of Professor Whitehead which deal brilliantly and sympathetically with traditional ideas. They have overlooked his acute penetration of the difference between the twentieth century and its predecessors.

Is this program a real reform, one adequate to the world crisis? Everything depends upon the supreme validity of western traditionalism. To express doubt

---

[8] *Adventures in Ideas* (The Macmillan Company, 1933), p. 117.

concerning the timeless validity of western tradition shocks the academic mind and in some circles leads to veiled innuendoes that the doubter is betraying his class — in this case, the learned class. The presupposition of learning in the western world is that wisdom was garnered into ancient Greece, transmitted to western Europe, passed in regular succession down the ages to the present and is next to spread around the globe. Therefore the business of learned men is to hand the torch to generations yet to come.

One simple fact must be made clear. The tradition of western man cannot be ignored in any conceivable educational system. But the question is not the ignoring of western tradition; the question is whether western tradition, or rather an educational program thus supremely given up to reviving and fortifying the younger college generation in the traditions of the west to such a degree that courses of this order shall be the only (or at least the principal) courses they are required to study, is the right reform for our day.

At the risk of an emotional shock to traditional loyalties it will be useful at this point to call on the reader for a supreme effort of the imagination. Let him suppose that an intelligent Oriental — a Hindu, a Chinaman, a Japanese, a Siamese — has had the courage to cast away politeness and to give his real opinion of the culture of western industrial society and of this return upon western traditionalism in edu-

cation. Told that these values, this philosophy, this religion descend from the Greeks and the Jews, told that
it is, or that it contains, an adequate philosophy of
life, catholic and universal, told that it is the shaping
force of modern culture and therefore the proper
study of our schools, what would such a person say?
I think he might speak in some bitterness of soul. I
think he might say something like this:

My western friends, your interpretation of man is,
to my way of thinking, marred by a fatal ambiguity.
This ambiguity arises from your simple-minded confusion of man universal with man in the western
world — and not only that, but western man only in
partial and intermittent aspects of his thought and
his activity. To us who live in other continents the
ambiguity of your tradition is more conspicuous than
its consistency.

For example, the central idea of this tradition, as I
understand it (he continues), is the greatest respect
for the individual, the greatest reverence for each human soul. If this is a real tradition operative within
your western history, why has this culture of yours
ruthlessly slaughtered more human beings than any
other culture in recorded time?

Your culture professes something called romantic
love and it professes to find in the family the corner-
stone of its social structure. You do not see, and your
wise men do not see, the inherent contradiction in

these two governing ideas. If you really want to find a culture founded on the family, study China. Your family tradition does not square with the facts of existence in your megapolitan civilization, nor does it square with your sexual mores. You cannot, as you do in your middle class tradition, confuse property right in a woman with romantic love; you cannot, as you do, confuse chastity with virtue, without engendering and continuing to engender emotional tensions, sexual maladjustments and neurotic personalities. Have not the art and literature of western culture, notably since the Renaissance, had as their principal theme the private unhappiness of men and women? Why do your philosophers, your poets, your psychologists, especially in the enlightened twentieth century, proclaim not once but many times that there is at the core of your culture a deep-seated spiritual and sexual maladjustment?

Your culture has many inventions, the creations of your technology, but its economic system works so crazily that it piles up consumer goods beyond the needs of the populace in one part of the world and ruthlessly enslaves and exploits the population in other portions. In my country we call this western imperialism.

You tell me, he says, that the core of this western tradition is rationalism. But if anything is true of your culture, it is not only that rationalism does not fortify your people against the evil emotions involved in race prejudice (we know, we Orientals), national bias (that, too, we know) and cultural parochialism (and my speaking as I do is pertinent to this issue), but it actually provides weapons for weakening the critical intelligence your education theoretically exists to train. I refer to the emotional propaganda in which you bathe your western masses. The radio, the movie, the press, the magazine and, above all, your western advertising, upon which you annually spend billions of dollars in order to drug all discrimination — here, indeed, is the final irony of your cultural development.

I know (he concludes) that there are many good and great men among you. I do not claim that our sages are wiser than yours. I do not deny that the defects of your civilization would also arouse the indignation of wise men in your tradition from Plato to the present, nor do I deny that studying the texts of these men may do something to call the attention of a minority of your people to the evils of your society. But as you have in the past adjudged us by the fruits of our culture — we are the "heathen" you sought to convert — so we in turn judge you by the fruits of your culture as we have seen it in the East. We owe you much, both good and evil, but the fruit of twenty centuries of western culture, as we see it, is the bankruptcy of the west and the hatred and envy sown by western imperialism. Unfortunately, from our point of view, the bomb dropped on Hiroshima was simply the latest of the destructive products of your civilization.

Such, or something like it is the searing indictment of western tradition a candid Oriental might utter. Let us grant he overstates his points. Let us grant his utterance is one-sided. Let us claim for the west and for western thought everything that can be legitimately claimed for it. It will still be true that an educational preoccupation with western philosophy, western science and western values will do nothing to explain to westerners why, by other parts of the world, western culture is viewed with deep distrust. Moreover, nothing in the proposed program permits the western student to discover why the Oriental persists in the strange error of regarding himself as also a person of refinement, of ethical standards and of religious values.

If then the inference is fair that a tree is known by its fruits, and if twenty-five centuries of western tradition eventuate in imperialism, fascism and frustration so great that Europe, incapable of saving itself from destruction, has had to call upon the British Commonwealth of Nations, Russia and the United States for aid, one can only inquire with the supposititious candid Oriental why the tradition of western learning, supposed to be synonymous with world-wide wisdom, has proved so weak. The answer of the learned is curious.

The answer is that the troubles lie, not with the tradition, but with human beings who will not live in the glory and wisdom of the tradition. Therefore the tradition must be retaught. But if, after twenty-five centuries, the tradition has not succeeded in persuading a sufficient number of leading westerners to live by its light, one can only remark that either the tradition lacks something or that men are incapable of absorbing its wisdom. Perhaps, however, western tradition is not enough.

Any reader of Eric Fischer's thoughtful book, *The Passing of the European Age*, the thesis of which is confirmed by all demographical predictions, must have been forced to recognize that in Mr. Wendell Willkie's "One World," the European tradition is no longer central. As Dr. Fischer sadly writes:

> The shift of the centers of gravity will merely be accelerated if Europe collapses. This shift will continue even in case Europe should recover. Europe can never regain the position it maintained during the last two centuries. We feel entitled to state that the Age of Europe has passed.[9]

The question is not whether Greece or Judaea has passed, leaving its wisdom behind for the study of mankind; the question is whether in a world in which Europe counts for less and less, European wisdom is

[9] *The Passing of the European Age* (Harvard University Press, 1943), p. 201.

enough. What Dr. Fischer has said has been said by others before him — by Spengler and H. G. Wells among others. A similar lesson is reiterated in more affirmative terms in F. S. C. Northrop's *The Meeting of East and West.*

When the rest of the globe is openly or covertly in rebellion against the fruits of Europeanism, to reorganize American higher education around a return to Europeanism would appear to be a dangerous revival of that ethnocentrism which makes the history of France of supreme importance to American youth but allows them totally to neglect the history of China except as the "Europeans opened it up." One is scarcely prepared to admit that renewing our intellectual and emotional attachment to that small fraction of the human race between the Vistula and the Bosphorus, and the English Channel and the Straits of Gibraltar is the sole effective reform in higher education. In view of the general complacency that has overwhelmed us since we helped our Allies to win a victory, this parochial return upon the past seems, indeed, positively harmful. If ever there was a time when we should learn what values, hopes and ambitions are cherished in the vast areas of Russia, the rest of Asia, Africa, South America and the islands of the sea, now, if ever is the time. The academic mind, one fears, has not adjusted itself to the full meaning of the post-atomic age.

FLIGHT FROM FEAR

FLIGHT FROM FEAR

The weakness of educational "reform" is that too much of it is verbal only, as any publisher of textbooks will in his confidential moments admit. Men alter words and think they have changed things. For example, if, in any given college, instruction has hitherto been offered by reasonably competent persons in Shakespeare, in Dante, in Aquinas and in Plato separately, nothing is essentially changed by assembling Shakespeare, Dante, Aquinas and Plato as a course in Great Books to be taught by one or more of the same persons who formerly offered instruction in these four authors individually, unless some radically new mode of interpretation or amalgamation has intervened. So, too, a course in the history of western institutions may, by omitting much historical matter, be simpler and in a specious sense clearer than a course in European history, a course in political science and a course in American history taken separately, but if the approach is historical still, if the intent is mainly to show how western institutions came into being, no radical reform has been made. The student has of course been strengthened in his belief that the western world has superior value.

As Professor Northrop somewhere says, "Clearly, a conflict cannot be resolved by reaffirming one of the factors which generate it," and the primary conflict of our time is the revolt against the results of twenty centuries of western culture.

A similar verbal difficulty clogs the present discussion. Every age likes to think of itself as unique. Part of that unique quality is that it faces a "crisis." The difficulty is therefore to distinguish between the word "crisis" in the worn sense and the tragic problem of our time. Academic men accustomed to the historical point of view tend to dissolve the problem of the twentieth century into the familiar constituents of historical "crises" of past time; they do not understand that when scientists (who do not on the whole take the historical point of view) proclaim that western civilization faces the most serious crisis in history, scientists mean precisely what they say.

But the discovery of the murderous potentialities in nuclear energy, together with the rapid invention of other death-dealing robot-like machines, is an event of absolute importance — an event of the same order of magnitude as the discovery of fire or the invention of the wheel, and not merely another "crisis" like the French Revolution or the Black Death. Education must somehow take account of events in a world in which Soviet Russia has become a dominant power, Asia is violently disturbed and man's uneasiness about his traditional values has spread from a few troubled spirits at the top of the social pyramid down among the mass of mankind everywhere. Merely to reaffirm past values by a return upon dead sages will not quite do. What we need is an educational program that will face the present with courage and interest.

The academic return upon the past which takes shape as either a demand for unity of dogma or a demand for tradition is, of course, comprehensible. It is part of that thirst for security which is a mark of our frightened age.

So far as the western world is concerned, it is possible to assume either that our culture is breaking up around us or that we are experiencing the pangs of a global revolution so vast, so profound and perhaps so incomprehensible that men — even educated men — do not want to face it and to try to estimate its causes, its direction or its possible end. The atom bomb is not the cause of this revolution, if it be one, but its latest result — a symptom of the profound dislocation of traditional securities in our technological culture. Western man has preoccupied himself with war as a continuing occupation, with the technology necessary for the waging of his complicated wars and with the nationalisms which are at once the cause and the consequence of the holocausts he makes. At length the disruption of social patterns which he causes is be-

come so evident that even in prosperous America men
are afraid.

We do not like to face the problem we have
created. We like to believe in the culture we are used
to. We cannot, if we are honest, believe that this culture is an absolute good and we must know, if we are
sensitive to opinion, that millions of other human beings in other continents do not like this culture but on
the contrary envy, hate or despise it. All this induces
fear and insecurity. When men no longer believe in
the culture which has maintained them, a psychology
of fear becomes central in their emotions and in their
actions. That psychology of fear is evident in the life
of western man. And when men are frightened they
seek security. They seek security, among other
places, in familiar educational patterns.

The most obvious form of this thirst for safety is
the demand for social security on the part of the
masses of western men, a demand that antagonizes
conservatives, including some academic economists,
who feel that their own security is threatened by the
unreasonable demands of others. The cry for social
security means that industrial culture, in contrast to
other cultures studied by anthropologists, is still so
careless of the single life that the little man, lacking
the safety of custom for his old age and lacking assurance that his children will have protection in case of
his illness or death, secures, as it were, the artificial

guarantees of legislation. Otherwise he believes that industry would throw him aside like a broken tool.

A second familiar form of this thirst for security is seen in the establishment by law of bonuses, pensions, preferences for jobs, hospitalization at government expense and other forms of protection for the millions who, whether they wanted to or not, were forced to serve in the vast armies of western society and who, on being discharged from these armies face the grim competition of the industrial order they fought to preserve. The soldiers who in the American Revolution created the republic were for the most part satisfied with gifts of land as patriotic largesse. But beginning with the Civil War and thereafter in increasing degree, the discharged veteran has demanded and secured a variety of guarantees against want, unknown to previous history and intended to stifle his gnawing fear of being cast aside as was the eighteenth century soldier pictured in Goldsmith or Smollett.

A third form of this fear is a flight from that very rationalism which created the industrial order. This flight may be into some form of religious mysticism — the number of cults arising in the western world during the last three centuries is, indeed, surprising; or it may be a flight from the responsibilities (and therefore from the uncertainties) of freedom, into social mysticism, as Erich Fromm points out in his *Escape From Freedom*. The most glaring instance is of course the case of the Nazi state. In that state the little man, conscious of his insignificance and his mortality, secured a fleeting sense of security by identifying himself with the deathless commonwealth. Fascism is but an exaggerated form of that passionate self-identification with one's own people, with one's own culture and with one's own folkways which is evident in the hysterical nationalism of our time.

The relevance of these examples of this search for security, to educational problems is that in a culture thus avid for reassurance, education experiences similar hopes and fears. The search for educational reassurance represented by the programs just discussed rightly sees that there is wisdom in past time. Indeed, in view of the fact that the departments most concerned with these programs — philosophy, history, the languages and literatures in one group, and the social sciences in another — tend to view the world historically and tend to be satisfied that a genetic study of any institution is both a defense and an evaluation of it, one is not surprised to find this disinclination to face forward until the past has been thoroughly explored. The scientific departments, to whom history is of small interest, have, as we have seen, only a minor part in these educational changes. But the citation of Cicero's sentence that he who knows only the present remains a child is scarcely an adequate answer to the fact that students have only the present — the sacred present, in Whitehead's phrase — in which to live; and the sobering fact remains that, whatever virtues these programs possess, they are not conceived in a spirit of intellectual daring and they do not face the full challenge of the present era.

Neither the authoritarian programs nor the traditionalist one seems to be much interested in the educational tradition of the United States except to dwell upon its obvious errors. They do not give much space to the empirical method which, in some sense, created the unique experiment of public education in this country, converted the great state universities into the social and scientific laboratories they have become and carried the research method to a pitch of perfection unparalleled in world history. The appeal, indeed, is away from the American spirit of boldness and ingenuity. It is an appeal from John Dewey to the medieval Aristotle, from William James to Plato, from Horace Mann to Thomas Aquinas. The innovations are an answer to the cry for guidance, but they confuse means with ends. Books are instruments, not absolutes, and will not equip young Americans with a philosophy of life if the teachers have no philosophy. But the two branches of the proposed reform exhibit, the one an obsolescent authoritarianism foreign to American mores, the other, a timid and academic eclecticism. When we ask ourselves why leaders of academic education thus turn their backs upon the American experiment, the answer is complicated. The defects of that experiment are great and manifest. But no small part of the answer must be academic insecurity.

Desire for security among professors is as understandable as the desire for security among other Americans in a troubled era. Among college people the incidence of economic insecurity is high, despite the work of the American Association of University Professors. Moreover, for the last fifteen or twenty years the colleges as institutions have been tossed on the seas of depression, the draft, war, government control, federal subsidy of returning veterans, and demands for vocational training. Faculty members who went into government service are tired and want to resume their normal ways; and faculty members who stayed in the colleges and taught round the clock before, during and after the war are, if anything, more fatigued as a group than colleagues who had the stimulus of military contact. The intellectual climate of the last two decades has not been conducive to genuinely philosophic thought on educational problems. It somehow seems easier in an uncertain world to sink back into the comfortable arms of history. Moreover, the brilliant successes of science in devising new technological weapons is in such contrast to the failure of democratic culture in trying to reconstitute

Germany according to philosophical postulates which ought theoretically to be immediately acceptable to all men, that sensitive, book-minded persons prefer asking what Plato would say about the state to inquiring why we do not succeed in implanting in the German nation a zeal for American democracy. But the discrepancy between our science, fully committed to experimental research, and the arts and philosophy giving up experimentalism in favor of one or another pattern of "general" (and inevitably, in greater or less degree, dogmatic) education does not increase one's educational faith. The split is too obvious.

These are harsh words, and they are written with regret. Perhaps I can make my point clearer if I ask the reader to contrast the spirit of Soviet education with that of the educators we have been discussing. I have not a doubt that there are a great many things wrong with the Russian schools, and I have no doubt also that my discussion, so far, of present programs of academic innovation in this country is one-sided, prejudiced and blind to many virtues. Nevertheless, unless most observers are wrong, the spirit of Soviet education is joyous and affirmative. Whatever its bias, it succeeds in conveying to its young people a positive security, a sense that they are important to their own culture and that their culture is important to them here and now, and not as the detritus of historical cultures in past time. Call this attitude uncritical if you will, say if you like that the history taught Russian youth is unobjective, declare if you must that the Soviet Union is an intellectual despotism in which nobody dares to question the absolute rightness of communistic society, nevertheless the young people of Russia, a country that has suffered far more deeply and tragically in the last fifty years than has the United States, do not feel that their culture is sick and do not have to turn away from the present to discover the core of a good education. Is it unreasonable to ask that American democracy ought to produce something at least as stimulating?

In the Russian state the dynamic of culture apparently continues in war and peace alike, at least for our time. In the United States our cultural dynamic comes in spasms. During the late war we were capable of furious and concentrated energy. But this energy has been followed by a slump. Part of that decline is caused by the familiar operations of postwar psychology. Hostilities being over, the veteran in uniform longs impatiently for civilian life, which takes on in memory a haze of romantic perfection; but, once discharged, after a brief interval, he misses the emotional identification of himself with the group, which he experienced in the armed forces. By and by he transfers to his military or naval memories the attributes of perfection that formerly he gave to civilian life and in the meantime, as a substitute for this group action, joins the American Legion, the American Veterans Committee or any other group operative within the domain of his military memories.

This period of psychological readjustment should not be mistaken for a permanent cultural pattern. Nevertheless, World War II was not an ordinary war. It was a genuine question whether the democratic state could survive. If, after a reasonable period, the younger generation do not secure from industrial society the satisfactions they desire, the demand for change will become imperative. If, for example, the postwar boom is followed by a great depression, as many think it will be, this demand will mount into some sort of action. In the world generally the fall of the fascist states, moreover, has left a kind of vacuum in beliefs, which must be filled; and if the democratic state has not the dynamic energy to draw to itself the affirmative allegiance of the younger generation in the United States and abroad, the democratic state will decline. The cure is not simple "patriotism." The task of education is, along with other institutions of that state, to furnish this dynamic. But it must be an intelligent dynamic; it must not, as too often it has done in the past, mistake our parochial content with "western tradition" for an affirmative creed; it must not, as American education too often does, confuse chauvinism with democracy; it must not, as education is charged with doing, confuse the snobbism of our industrial aristocracy and the traditional veneers of our genteel training with the essence of a sound, affirmative education. I confess I do not see in the programs of academic reform any vital treatment of education in a democracy; and the fact that eighty percent of the veterans enrolled in college and university demand some kind of vocational training seems to indicate that these flaccid returns upon history do not have the liveliness needed to fortify the democratic spirit in the democratic state.

II

One difficulty with educational programs is that they are never built for time but are always built for eternity. Each pedagogical reformer, convinced that he has found at last a changeless and enduring way of educating human nature, announces his program as a series of timeless absolutes. Every curriculum has an air of being built upon the impregnable rock of holy scripture; and, since academic institutions are highly conservative, the new curriculum, once alive and vital, when it becomes moribund, either changes slowly or changes not at all. Thus in the British Isles a curriculum for the public schools that had real vitality for the Renaissance lingered spinelessly into the eighteenth and nineteenth centuries, nor could all the wit and wisdom of persons as gifted as Sydney Smith, Thackeray, John Stuart Mill and Thomas Huxley easily effect a change. So in American schools and colleges what has been, by sheer power of endurance, takes on a patina of wisdom and must, in the minds of teachers, forever be. Consider as an example the confused and contradictory arguments for the retention of Greek and Latin in our schools and colleges. Or again, consider how the departmental organization of our college faculties, which has split them into little groups conducting little internecine wars, is regarded by most professors as something absolute and inescapable, whereas, as a matter of history, the departmental system is the creation of the last seventy or eighty years.

I do not have the wisdom to launch another educational reform. The suggestions for a reorientation of college studies which here follow are not absolute and for all time; they are intended as a temporary expedient, one that may conceivably get us through the next fifteen or twenty years. They lack any absolute philosophy like neo-Thomism; and they do not directly offer the student what I regard as the most serious educational demand in the United States at the moment, namely, a democratic dynamic as vital to the democratic state as the communist dynamic of education seems to be to Russia. The problem of that dynamic is a problem of immense complexity, which only a few philosophers — for example, Ralph Barton Perry — have directly attacked; and to distinguish the merely conventional in our studies from what is lively and useful, to separate the cunning manipulation of democratic phraseology by big business or by demagogues from a really useful democratic philosophy; to attempt here and now a reinterpretation of the seventeenth and eighteenth century postulates of the American state so that these postulates have genuine meaning in our megapolitan, heterogeneous, industrialized society — all this is a prodigious problem, the solution of which would take us far afield and which I do not feel competent to attempt. Moreover, we vaguely feel that if communism is an international force, democracy should be exportable also; but, as this discussion has hinted more than once, "democracy" in the United States cannot be automatically exported to Asia or the Balkans or Africa or, apparently, even to Germany and Italy. The struggles of France to retain political democracy differ so importantly from political behavior in the British Isles or the Scandinavias as to suggest that democracy, unlike communism, is a protean manifestation and should not be confused with congressional elections in Massachusetts or California. All this amounts to a problem of immense magnitude, a problem that requires extended study, a problem that we must solve both nationally and globally. But as we have scarcely begun the explication of this immense and baffling situation, I for one am not prepared here and now to utter any *obiter dicta* on the subject. Solemnly to declare that in the democratic state education should be sympathetic to democracy is to say little enough. I can only claim that the following suggestions for a program, pragmatically conceived, are delivered, I trust, in a spirit of global democracy.

I suggest, then, that American colleges ought to consider some such program as this:

1. Professional or vocational training for all.
2. The study of the theory of science and of the application of scientific discoveries to our technology.
3. The assumptions and workings of representative government, particularly in the United States and in the British Commonwealth of Nations.
4. The study of Russia.
5. The study of the Orient.
6. The study of personal relationships in modern society.

I repeat that this program is intended to get us through the next two or three decades; it is not meant for eternity.

1. *Professional or vocational training for all.* — Perhaps the most persistent illusion of those concerned for liberal education is that it has nothing to do with vocational or professional training and is con-

taminated by that training. Thus one finds theorists insisting upon the obsolete distinction descending from a slave-supported society that vocational or professional training is "servile" education. This is regarded as explicitly or implicitly hostile to "liberal" education, and every bit of time and ground that can be gained for "liberal" education from the time and ground of vocational or professional education is hailed with joy as a triumph over a common enemy of inferior intellectual status. The imputation of inferior intellectual status to vocational or professional training is astonishing, in view of the patent fact that medical students, law students, engineering students and other students who know their own minds, work about twice as hard as students in the liberal arts courses. Yet, under present conditions, two years of "general" or "liberal" education are made to precede professional or vocational specialization on the ground that these years furnish a broad foundation for the narrowing vocationalism that is to follow. Except in the artificial world of the college, the human being does not automatically switch from two years of one sort of training to two years of a diametrically opposite sort and at the same time bring to bear upon his new training the well-meant, but unfocussed, education of his first two years. "Broad" the first two years may be, but they are not broadening. This common semantic confusion haunts educational discussion.

In his *Education for Responsible Living* Wallace B. Donham, for twenty-three years dean of the Harvard Business School, reports on his experience with and observation of about 12,000 graduates of five hundred undergraduate colleges and technical schools. In recent years, he tells us, graduates of the liberal arts colleges constituted 50 per cent of students entering that school. Dean Donham makes a powerful plea for the right sort of liberal education. But of the present attitude of liberal arts colleges towards professional and vocational training he says:

> Their contribution must be powerful enough to balance the convincing demonstration seen all around us that science and scientific training, conceived as narrowly as they conceive themselves, accomplish much in important and obvious but material ways. They must show students the catastrophic consequences of the resulting over-emphasis on material progress. It is too bad that, instead of thoughtful analysis leading to such affirmative demonstration of useful values, the liberal-arts colleges have so generally taken the easy attitude of disclaiming any intent or desire to be useful — truly a pathetic defeatist attitude for the custodians of the highest values. . . .[1]

> Many, if not most, college students take part or all of their work as preparation for making a living. Why, so long as this is true, should any college take pride that students who come seeking a general education leave without securing any education which equips them with background habits and skills useful in either living or making a living? [2]

> In my observation, the liberal-arts graduate who stops with the A.B. and enters active life in many cases faces pathetic problems. Somehow he feels his training ought to prepare him

[1] Harvard University Press, 1944, p. 25.
[2] Page 33.

to do a better job in life but, judged by the difficulties of making a real start and the drifting process through which he frequently goes, it does not. Some colleges seem to glory in this fact. It is frequently stated that liberal-arts training gives cultural values, trains men for life; not to make a living. But cultural values fly out the window when men can't get and hold jobs, and little self-respect remains if they can't make a living. The gaps now left are too wide even for the ablest men.[3]

Dean Donham is speaking of the men; any one who has year after year seen the bewilderment of graduates of women's colleges (or women graduating from coeducational colleges) which have prepared them neither for domestic life nor for even elementary jobs in our business civilization must join his severe condemnation of an unfocussed "liberal" education. The instinct of the veterans now in colleges, most of whom demand vocational or professional training, is sounder than the theory of academic humanists. "Making a life" is a fine phrase. But you cannot in most cases "make a life" without first making a living. In the midst of a highly competitive society on the profits of whose institutions they live, it seems to me positively immoral for liberal arts colleges elaborately to pretend that their lofty purpose is to avoid soilure and that their graduates are not going to participate in the struggle which is the heart of the capitalist system.

Indeed, I think the claim of the colleges to serious attention would improve if, abandoning an attitude

[3] Page 35.

that descends from medieval and Renaissance social patterns, they would insist that no one should be allowed to enter their doors until he gave some reasonable assurance that he proposed to pursue a course of professional or vocational training. It is wonderful how, when the individual establishes such a goal, education comes into focus. The postponement of the necessity for such a decision by two years has left the student wandering aimlessly through freshman and sophomore courses unrelated to each other and meaningless to him, since his understandable attitude is that they are patiently to be endured until he is permitted to begin his real education. But if from the beginning of his college work — indeed, if possible, before beginning that work — the student is faced with the necessity of making an adult choice of occupation, it soon becomes possible for the college to deal with him as an adult. His professional or vocational training will not then be crowded into the last two years of a four-year curriculum, and his "liberal" education will not be administered in the vast and shoreless void of two years of drift; on the contrary, the two can be administered together, the practical necessities of the one will focus the theoretical implications of the other, and the deeper the student plunges into his professional or vocational work, the more clearly will he see the necessity of a governing philosophy. The present order of college work — elementary courses,

then advanced courses, then courses in specialization
— may, indeed, be logical but it violates every principle of human psychology.

The professional or vocational training desired of
the liberal arts college is of two sorts. Many professions — law and medicine are examples — require
two years of liberal arts work for admission to professional courses and would gladly see this work better
integrated with professional needs. The seven-year
curriculum combining work in Harvard College with
work in the Harvard Law School indicates that this
can be done. Other professions — for example, engineering — demand little of the liberal arts, but
would welcome more if that "more" could be made to
have meaning for the future engineer. But most liberal arts students who do not look forward to professions like these are, as a matter of fact, attending the
liberal arts college for vocational training and will
upon graduation launch into the fiercely competitive
society that is America. One may regret the fierce-
ness of the competition. One may, as I have done,
lament the prepotent influence of technology upon
education. But we do not cure a condition by pretending, as liberal arts colleges do, that it does not
exist. As Dean Donham acidly remarks: "Now, for
most men, liberal education stops on Commencement
Day." Liberal education would begin for these same
men long before commencement day if the liberal arts

colleges, recognizing the vocational aims of the overwhelming majority of their students, would integrate "general education" with vocational training. One would, indeed, suppose that the pathetic belief of professional schools in the liberal arts would be immensely flattering to liberal arts faculties. Even under the programs of reforms we have discussed, these faculties make no attempt to study the nature of the vocational needs of their students but insist that whatever the faculty teaches is a private, mystical and absolute good in itself.

2. *The theory of science and the application of scientific discoveries to our technology.* Professional, vocational, technical or technological training — call it what you will — is unavoidable in a fiercely competitive industrial democracy. The problem is not to deny its necessity but to control and guide its force. The problem is to bring our social engineering up to the maturity of our technological engineering. The soundest element in the programs of general education now being adopted by liberal arts colleges is instruction in science — not in particular sciences, not in the metaphysics of scientific philosophy, but in the ordinary working assumptions of the scientific method; for example, controlled variables, verification, inference, and the like. This is certainly a step in advance of those beginning courses in chemistry, physics, biology or what not usually taught as if the be-

ginner were going to become a professional research worker.

But a course in "general science," a course in the history of science, a course in the postulates of the scientific method will merely increase our technological confusion unless it is joined to something else. That something else is the study of what happens to scientific discoveries when they are practically put to work in our industrial culture. The woeful gap presently existing between the physical and natural scientists and the engineers on the one hand and the economists, sociologists, psychologists and anthropologists on the other hand is the most distressing fissure in our education as it is in our society. That as many persons as possible living in a technological culture should know as much as possible about the working assumptions of the scientist is patent — so patent, it is embarrassing that education has taken thus long to make this discovery of the obvious; but that the spread of this information, unless it is positively checked by other, sobering, social forces may merely speed our descent into the maelstrom is also so patent as scarcely to require demonstration. Scientists, many of them, are genuinely distressed at the cultural lag between their work and the imperfections of the social processes which use the results of their labors; yet a movement like Science Search, intended to discover scientific talent in the secondary schools and encourage it to enter research training, merely increases the rapidity of our technological advance without guaranteeing any concomitant social understanding. Economist and sociologist, psychologist and anthropologist must, in my judgment, join the scientist and point out that when science invents the internal combustion engine, vast economic and sociological forces are set to work. It is insufficient to praise research for its own sake. The tremendous (and sometimes tragic) results of research for its own sake, when these results take the form of widespread technological change in modern society, are as basic to an understanding of the modern world as any part of scientific theory. The creation of instructional units of this sort will be a matter of great difficulty, but to keep scientific theory in one compartment and economic and social studies of a technological culture in another compartment is precisely the tragic error of our education and of our culture.

3. *Representative government in the United States and in the British Commonwealth of Nations.* Doubtless there is something to be said for a general history of western institutions or of Europe or of the western world or whatever other formula is advanced in programs of general education. I cannot escape feeling that, however fruitful such instruction may be for philosophers, as an element of common education during the next two decades or so a critical study of

362478

the history and function of representative government in this country and in the British Commonwealth
of Nations is far more necessary. What are its real
strength and weakness? Why does it seem to break
down in most of the countries of the earth and why
does it not perform more effectively for us? As I have
indicated, the fond assumption of western man that
British parliamentarianism or the American check-
and-balance system is both an absolute good and
something for the export trade is one of the dangerous
historical illusions of our day. If all undergraduates
had time and interest enough, general courses in history might, indeed, throw light upon the problem of
the democratic state, but history, to have general
meaning, must for most students be focussed upon
present problems; and the present problem with us is
whether our country can survive under an eighteenth
century constitution operative on nineteenth century
postulates in the "One World" of the twentieth century. If the world during the next few years is going
to be split, as it threatens to be, between the communistic and the democratic theories of the state,
surely our common studies should be far more real-
istically focussed upon the workings of the principal
democratic states in our tradition. This seems to me
so elementary I do not think it requires elaborate explication.

4. *The study of Russia.* The same logic, however,

makes the study of Russia — its culture, its government, its economic structure, the character and desires of its myriad peoples — of paramount importance, and it is gratifying to see a slow increase of
academic interest in Russian studies. If Russia is to
become the chief enemy of the democracies (which
God forbid!) we ought to comprehend her; if she is
to become the friend and aider of the democracies, all
the more reason for the widest spread of sympathetic
information about the Russian empire. In the next
quarter of a century this empire is going to be of far
greater importance to modern man than the empire of
the Caesars or of Charlemagne or of Napoleon, now
commonly studied in the schools. It is high time the
Americans got over their silly attitude toward "communism" and tried to comprehend it. Even sons of
members of the National Association of Manufac-
turers are going to have to understand the workings
of the Russian state system.

Of course it takes a certain courage to advocate a
sympathetic approach to the Russian problem. Not
long ago, when Cornell University founded a school of
Russian studies, hysteria swept through the conservative or reactionary New York press. The same educational timidity which in World War I crippled the
American war effort by throwing the German language out of the schools on the ground that it was an
enemy tongue is, alas! already at work among us,

thwarting the spread of elementary information about the Russian state. This vast nation shares with the English-speaking nations the domination of the globe; the average American student knows less about it than he knows about Julius Caesar or Cromwell. We cannot continue indefinitely the policy of ignoring what we fear or dislike. Every consideration — the importance of the Russian theory of economic life, business interest, politics, the life of the arts, the advance of science, gratitude, the solution of the problem of racial tension, geography, diplomacy, the operations of the United Nations charter — demands a primary place in American education for the study and comprehension of the Russian world.

5. *The study of the Orient.* The westward course of the American empire did not halt at the Golden Gate but has gone on to Hawaii, the Philippines, Japan, China, India, and Asia generally. Asia is the problem of the future, a problem we have done as much as any other nation to create and which we must do as much as any other nation to solve. It is at least probable that by sheer force of numbers, if mankind is to survive, the future of mankind lies with the Asiatics. They are, and they will remain, numerously the greatest single segment of the human race. American undergraduates know nothing or next to nothing about the cultures, the history, the problems and the needs of these myriads with whom American inter-

course is bound constantly to increase. The wide-spread lack of comprehension of even the simplest postulate of any Oriental civilization, the profound disruption wrought in the Orient by the crude forcing process of "Occidentalization" hitherto common, the rich contribution which the Orient has to make to our troubled western world — these and multiple other considerations demand that if the United States is a world power in a global universe, its educational system cannot longer ignore Oriental culture as it has done hitherto except at rarefied scholarly levels. Chinese universities as a matter of course require the study of the West; we in our blindness do not think the East worth study. Yet, together with Russia, it is the most important cultural problem our technological civilization has to face.

Perhaps the words of Professor Northrop in *The Meeting of East and West*, may carry conviction if mine do not:

The time is here when we must understand the Orient if we would understand ourselves, and when we must learn how to combine Oriental and Occidental values if further tragedy, bitterness, and bloodshed are not to ensue.[4]

These considerations all remind us that neither war nor the peace-time problems of our world can be diagnosed as a simple issue between the good and the bad. This, to be sure, is the interpretation which each party to the disputes of our time puts upon events. But the very number and diversity of conceptions of what the good and the divine is give the lie to any such diagnosis, and to the ever present proposal that a return to

[4] The Macmillan Company, 1946, p. 4.

the traditional morality and religion is the cure for our ills. All that such proposals accomplish is the return of each person, each religious denomination, each political group or nation to its own pet traditional doctrine. And since this doctrine (or the sentiments which it has conditioned) varies at essential points from person to person, group to group, nation to nation, and East to West, this emphasis upon traditional religion and morality generates conflicts and thus intensifies rather than solves our problems. This in fact is the basic paradox of our time; our religion, our morality and our "sound" economic and political theory tend to destroy the state of affairs they aim to achieve.[5]

This condition will expectably increase in complexity and intensity, because in addition to continuing conflict between diverse moral, religious, political and economic ideologies in the West, there will be a more direct confrontation of Occidental cultural values.

Nevertheless, to become aware of this complicated, dangerous, and paradoxically confusing situation is to have at hand the clue to the way to meet it.[6]

At a very high level Professor Northrop's book shows how the conflict of cultures can be made educationally understandable. What is needed — what is desperately needed in our colleges — is a simplification and a generalization of his courageous volume.

6. *The study of personal relationships in modern society.* The elements of general education hitherto suggested may prove difficult in the teaching, but they are at any rate specific. The sixth and last of these elements, highly important though it is, cannot be so specific. I refer to the need of restoring confidence in the relations between man and man.

[5] Pages 5–6.   [6] Page 6.

Perhaps, in a fiercely competitive society, confidence in these relations cannot be wholly restored, but the present corruption of these relations can certainly be checked and the condition improved. The deepest corruption of western life — a corruption revealed by the Nazis only because they exaggerated a tendency everywhere seen in the industrial order — is the profound distrust of personal relationships within that order. The logic of the Nazi state came to be that nobody trusted anybody else. Before we conclude that, by destroying Hitler, we have destroyed the inner weakness of western society, let us ask ourselves how far the sense of insecurity has spread. The common phrases of the day are illuminating. The fear of being double-crossed, the fear of sticking your neck out, the fear of being taken in, the fear, in sum, that your competitor may not play the game according to the rules — these are the fears that seem to haunt our young men and women as they enter the competitive game. One of the most illuminating facts to be observed in this connection is the way many of these younger persons turn to psychology and to anthropology for a more valid explanation of the vagaries of human behavior than is to be found in the official sanctions of that behavior.

The calm good faith of the younger Russian generation in each other and in their culture is in contrast to the uneasiness evident in the American world lest personal relations, business relations, labor relations, or any other of a dozen connections between individual and individual shall prove deceptive. We are each one afraid of being "worked." To repeat Professor Mayo's words: "we have in fact passed beyond that stage of human organization in which effective communication and collaboration were secured by established routines of relationship." Perhaps the most tremendous task before higher education is to seek out means of restoring between human being and human being that calm and confident relationship which our western culture has lost, is losing, and will continue to lose until psychologist and physician, sociologist and anthropologist, by combining their studies, can perhaps restore this simple faith to western man. Professor Mayo rightly charges us with "utter social incompetence." But the beginning of social competence is the trust of man in man; and a wider understanding of the psychology of personal relationships seems to me a more desperate need in our education than polite courses in literature, philosophy and the fine arts. The spirit of scepticism and disillusion which seems to charm many specialists in these latter fields is, however, sorry guarantee for the restoration of confidence; and it may be that nothing short of a renovation of belief in the democratic process will cure our humanists. "Physician, heal thyself" was never more applicable.

WHO IS AS THE WISE MAN?

WHO IS AS THE WISE MAN?

Discussing "The New Weapons" in *The New York Times* for June 30, 1946, immediately after the Bikini experiment, the conservative Hanson W. Baldwin thus ended his article:

The Cassandras and the professional pessimists have been predicting for generations that each new war would mean the end of civilization or the extinction of man; each new weapon has always been hailed as "absolute." Yet life and civilization have endured.

Nevertheless, ever since the industrial revolution, wars have become more and more total, weapons more and more powerful. The technological revolution is bringing this trend to its dreadful climax, a climax in which large parts of great cities can be smashed by one atomic bomb, a climax in which oceans, mountain ranges, terrain barriers and distance itself can be easily spanned by long-range missiles.

Any future war, therefore, is bound to be more dreadful than wars of the past. A new conflict will not spell the end of civilization or the extinction of man, for man is a peculiarly tenacious animal, and civilization will endure as long as there is a library in Peru or Afghanistan or Siam. But another war will surely mean the death of millions and perhaps the end of certain civilizations, and it may cause the reversion of a large part of earth to the Dark Ages.

Such is the danger of the mechanism which man has created. Whether "civilization" will endure because there may be books in Afghanistan, whether "the end of certain civilizations" means in fact the end of western industrial culture is unimportant as a form of words, and I do not desire to debate Mr. Baldwin on minor problems of logic and style. The problem is what higher education can do as it confronts the monster that higher education has, through its technological training, helped to create. My contention is that current theories of academic reform are inadequate to the tragic situation of our world; and I have ventured to suggest as a temporary program to replace these genteel dogmas a set of problems to be solved in the spirit of the American educational tradition. Despite the danger of feeding our sense of complacency, the practical importance of continuing the experimental and forward-going spirit of that education seems to me to outweigh the theoretical desirability of a return to the Catholic church, a return to the medieval university, a return to a selected list of books or a return to the "traditions of western culture." We are used to the American mode in education. Provided we do not think the whole world should be either Americanized or Occidentalized, we can use the American mode in education wisely for cosmopolitan ends.

Basing itself, then, upon the American habit of solving problems empirically, the program just outlined is not an absolute, but something temporary and experimental, to be modified in practice and eventually to be supplanted by something better. Indeed, my hope is that it will be so supplanted. My hope is that in the next two decades philosophers, psychologists and educators will have discovered practicable ways to teach democracy as a cultural dynamic to the United States. This is perhaps the most difficult pedagogical problem before us.

We have seen in the fascist states the disastrous results of indoctrinating a younger generation with a fallacious absolute and of training them uncritically to accept whatever the state tells them to believe. Democratic critics of contemporary Russia are certainly right in saying that, however excellently the Soviet system may solve the problem of economic democracy, in that state intellectual democracy (in the sense of intellectual freedom) is severely curtailed. Moreover, the teaching of "democracy" in the United States, a nation which as time goes on grows more and more rigid and conservative, is more than likely, unless educators exhibit courage and intelligence, to become synonymous with the most vicious form of chauvinism. Already the pressure to teach "Americanism" is one aspect of the arrant nationalism prevalent in our unhappy half century.

In view of our need for a cultural dynamic we cannot postpone the problem indefinitely. That problem is to find some practical, popular means of combining two disparate elements, each involved in emotion, into a single educational aim which shall receive

both critical and emotional loyalty: the implanting
in the younger generation of a real enthusiasm for
the theory and practice of democracy; and the securing at the same time a real and an intelligent toleration of other outlooks than the western one, provided that these philosophies are not aggressive and
authoritarian. All this demands a profound readjustment of attitudes and evaluations — how great a readjustment and re-education readers of Professor
Northrop's book will discover.[1] How to accomplish
this task is the dominant educational problem of the
United States in the twentieth century, one that must
be solved by more vigorous tactics than a simple return upon the past of western man.

This book is open to the charge of seeming to postpone the solution. But the more limited, immediate
and, if you will, empirical program here outlined at
least has the advantage of leading into the problem of
a dynamic democratic culture and not away from it.
It is here contended that the six suggested aims for
the liberal college really confront the contemporary
world and really challenge the living interests of most
undergraduates. The first and sixth points deal directly with the insecurity that haunts them — the
first (a candid recognition of the preponderant force
of professional or vocational training), by recogniz-

[1] Americans should especially ponder the significance of his chapter
on "The Free Culture of the United States" in *The Meeting of East and
West.*

ing the truth that in competitive capitalism a diffuse
and unfocussed education, despite exceptions of great
brilliance, handicaps the competitor if he has to start
from scratch; the other (the problem of personal relations in our sick society), by attacking directly one
of the chief sources of our insecurity. The other
planks in the platform — science and its actual social
applications, the question of representative government, the problem of Russia and the problem of the
Orient — really illumine the difficult society into
which the younger generation is plunged on leaving
college. My hope is that by interweaving professional
or vocational education with these philosophic and
social problems of immediate cogency, instead of
postponing that education until a theoretical "broad"
base has been laid, we shall succeed in really putting
philosophic and social considerations to work.

II

A thousand objections immediately arise. "General" or "liberal" education has usually been thought
of in formal terms like philosophy, literature, the
arts, the sciences, and of right combination among
these traditional elements of the college curriculum.
The program here outlined as basically desirable says
nothing about literature and philosophy and science,
except incidentally. How can one be sure that the
right balance is maintained? How can one be sure

that one is not turning out badly educated men and women unless one demands a certain quantum of literature and philosophy and science?

The tacit assumption of this comment is that existing curricula with their formal requirements of concentration and distribution and their formal logical structures succeed in producing cultivated graduates in the humanistic sense of the word. Attendance upon any alumni gathering is a sufficient practical comment upon this assumption. Aesthetic, literary or philosophical lore is as a matter of fact not taught except to a relative minority with any such effectiveness as is professional or vocational training; and however fondly the alumnus may look back upon his dear old college days, it is rather upon an agreeable and harmless utopia than upon the source of a cultural dynamic in his own life. The difficulty with the genteel college is that it remains genteel. "Culture" is something for one's leisure hours, for women, for librarians and for other minority groups. The difficulty is that books read in a vacuum, philosophy taught formally, history as a requirement and science as a required balance to intellectual digestion have a somewhat remote significance for one's later life except to a minority of scholarly or aesthetic temperaments.

Nothing, indeed, more illumines the theoretical approach of the academic mind to the painful problem

of values than the question of books, which may here
serve as an exposition of why so much college instruction is superficial. To the aesthetic or the book-
minded person a classic is a work of stimulating
interest, filled with thought about man and the universe, enriched with the patina of history, and beau-
tiful with traditional form and modulated style. What
can be more simple and right than, by requiring the
young idea to read this work under skillful guidance,
to enrich the budding personality through canalizing
the wealth of the classic into the personality being
shaped by instruction and reading? And the professor of English (and concurrently of any other
bookish branch of the curriculum) points with justi-
fiable pride to students of his who have been awak-
ened to literary glories, who have learned to "love
books" in college or who have perhaps gone on into
the graduate school as a result of this affectionate instruction. All men can, in greater or less degree,
profit by the classics. Only — there is the unfortunate
unbookish quality of the alumni reunion, from which
the professor of English flees and towards which his
attitude is one of enforced toleration. Why does not
learning to "love books" seem to have more durable
effects than it does?

It would require a volume larger than this to ex-
plore the truth and error mingled in the theory. Suffice it to say that the meaning of any book lies in its

relevance to the reader at the time he reads it. A book of ephemeral value may be extremely cogent and, contrariwise, as college courses in literature frequently show, the great classics may have only a formal, not a living, significance. Indeed, with the vast majority of undergraduates, this formal quality is all that the classics ever possess. In truth, the great classic, product usually of a mature mind which has known the sweat and agony of existence, is remote in actuality from the slight experience, the limited emotional range and the simple intellectual equipment of most college students. The surprising thing in truth is not that the classics too frequently remain inert matter, but that the energy of teachers brings many of them into a real, if fitful, life in the classroom. Unfortunately this life too seldom extends beyond the artifices of course instruction.

All this is not to argue that the classics are not to be taught. It is to say, however, that books have meaning in life or in pedagogy only when, as Williams James would say, the student faces a real option; and in a world that must either unite or perish, so far as classroom instruction can furnish the semblance of reality, the real options that most students are going to confront are of the sort outlined in the program of general education herein laid down. How far does any book throw light upon the problem of representative (or, if you will, popular) government? What can we learn from the classics of Orient and Occident about living issues East and West? What has Shakespeare or Emerson to tell us about the validity of personal relationships? Curricula do not exist for the sake of books, of philosophy professors, of history texts or even of science; on the contrary, science and the arts exist for the sake of a curriculum relevant to the needs of a society supporting the college. The academic mind is always pretending that "real life" fails in proportion as it does not mirror academic order.

A second objection is that the program demands the study of Russian and of Oriental culture but does not equally demand the study of western culture. This is true. Had we but time and space enough, everything from Cretan civilization to Bikini could be brought to bear upon modern problems. If one supposes that the program here suggested ignores the traditions of western culture (which it does not), I should still defend it on two grounds: first, that the urgency of our times gives priority to the kind of study I have suggested; and second, that in education we must take some things for granted. Surely, unless secondary education is a complete failure, the student has learned enough about the backgrounds of the western world so that he does not feel alien in it. Surely the student intelligent enough to be admitted to college has learned from high school, from newspaper and magazine, from radio and movie at least enough to get along. That "enough" is, I grant, erratic, wrong-headed and ill-organized; and college teachers take perpetual delight in dwelling upon the absurd historical errors and ignorances of the young. But the weakness of the academic mind is the study of perfection; and as between the lamentable incorrectness of undergraduate information about Pericles or the middle ages, Matthew Arnold or Dante, the categorical imperative or solipsism, and the lack of any information whatsoever about the peoples and nations on most of the surface of the globe, for the next twenty years or so I am willing to risk misinformation about Pericles and French classicism in order to gain at least a modicum of information about Russia, the Orient, and other pressing matters. If this be philistinism, make the most of it.

The program here proposed does not concentrate upon the traditions of western history, but neither does it ignore the West. On the contrary, it concentrates upon four highly essential elements in western civilization. Professional, technological or vocational training for skilled or specialized jobs is one of the prime qualities differentiating western culture from traditional Oriental notions of education. If the development of industrial culture has, as it obviously has, led to the curious and disheartening breakdown in the validity of personal relationships, then the

study of why these relationships too often fail western man lies at the heart of the western cultural problem. Any catalog of the most characteristic produc-
tions of western civilization will certainly include
western science and representative government —
both are here included, and my proposal to make the
assumptions of science clearer to more people goes
beyond the claims of traditionalists in that it is proposed also to make clear what happens to a society in
which science constantly receives new practical applications. One must not confuse book learning satisfactory in the library with a genuine operational grasp
of western culture. And eventually, as I have indicated, I hope that philosophers, educators and psychologists will work out a philosophically based dynamic for democratic society that is not found in any
program hitherto set up.

A third objection partially includes the previous
two. It arises from the absence of customary terms of
academic reference. What about departments? What
about degree programs? What place for chemistry
or mathematics, foreign language and composition?
Is this culture? Is this a liberal education?

I have deliberately avoided all mention of departments and their specialties in connection with this
program for a particular reason. Departments are,
by and large, one of the two greatest evils in our
academic education, the present conduct of graduate

schools being the other. Unless and until we abandon
the double-entry book-keeping by which in departments we now appoint, promote, pay and subdue our
teachers, it really makes no great difference whether
we adopt the dogmatic system or fall back upon the
traditions of western culture or take over the ideas
here suggested, because, in the classic phrase of Al
Smith, slice it any way you will, it will still be ba-
loney. We cannot make real educational advance, so
far as general training is concerned, without over-
hauling the departmental system.

The present departmental organization of the
American college faculty represents, indeed, the inherent contradiction in the aims of that college and
may be insoluble. Departments are the products of
specialism, which they in turn nourish; specialism is
part of the professional or vocational training necessary for survival in capitalist society; and yet specialism, unduly emphasized, is, as traditionalists rightly
aver, at war with every sound conception of education or the state. On the other hand, the faculty of
the liberal arts and sciences theoretically represents
the wholeness of modern knowledge outside the professions; men therefore turn to it for the general
training they desiderate. But the college professor
cannot serve two masters; he cannot operate simultaneously on the level of "broad" general training and
on the level of specialism, inasmuch as his own profes-

sional training, his professional loyalty and his professional business are part of the very specialism he is supposed to counteract; and the result is the uneasy compromise of the American college program. The roots of this evil go back to the graduate school, to which I shall by and by turn; here I can only point to the dilemma of all programs of curricular reform.

The situation is difficult and may be insoluble; it is not yet hopeless. Perhaps the most fruitful educational experience coming out of World War II was the discovery that, under stress, departmentalism can be made to curl up and die. In place of the artificial structures of "departments," in surprising degree the creatures of college book-keeping and the bane of administration, there were established during the war what were known as area and language schools. That is to say, the colleges brought to bear upon the interpretation of a given culture — Japan will do for illustration — *any* person and *any* information that were relevant, whether they had to do with economics or dating statues of Buddha or identifying volcanic ash or memorizing verbs. What is here proposed for peace is simply the continuation and amplification of this program. In place of dividing Russia among a dozen hostile departments — Slavic languages, geography, history, economics, fine arts, and the like — we ought to bring to bear upon the interpretation of Russia for general education whatever specialties, whatever disciplines, whatever knowledges illumine the problem. Similarly for other topics — the interpretation of scientific method and the application of science in social terms, the history of representative government, the cultures of the Orient, the problem of personal relationships. I do not see that the problem of personnel organization is greater in peace than it was in war; and as the only alternative to this regrouping of teachers is apparently the continuation of the departmental system, I prefer experimentation. One is told, of course, that it can't be done. The reply is that it has been done, and done successfully. I do not see that the administrative problem is more complicated in peace than in war. I am not utopian enough to think that the evils of academic organization are completely to be remedied; what I do argue is that it is more important for American undergraduates to understand Russia and representative government, science, personal relations and the cultures of the East than it is to perpetuate a scholarly hierarchy. One sadly reflects again, however, that no priesthood is ever reformed by its members.

A fourth objection to the program is that it is too hard. What? Undergraduates to study the Orient? And Russia? And the development of representative government here and abroad, the techniques and application of science, and the problem of relationships in industrial society? Well, I think better of students than objectors do. My uneasiness is not for the student but for the teacher. I am willing to wager that, once the undergraduate discovers the relevancy of the proposed program (or something like it) to the world he lives in, he will bring to it a zeal beyond that he casually lends to conventional college courses and beyond the more active interest an undergraduate minority of a highly literate order brings, it is said, to the study of Great Books. Moreover, the scattered parts of my studies are already present and being pursued in the curriculum — for example, the theory of science and the Brito-American problem of government; all I seek is to bring these scattered parts out from under the departmental system into living wholes for at least the next two decades.

American students are, I think, at least as intelligent as Orientals. I have observed for a good many years that Oriental students manage to familiarize themselves with western culture that is to them at least as difficult as Oriental and Russian cultures seem to be to Americans. I do not see that it is any harder to study the problems proposed than it is to master the scientific and other classics solemnly proposed in the St. John's curriculum, supposing these to be really mastered. The truth is, of course, that the theoretical demands of the conventional college curriculum are high; they are not enforceable because they do not seem to students essential. I hope to make some of these demands essential by giving them reality. Learning and mastery will follow upon interest, precisely as it does in vocational or professional training.

A fifth objection is the vagueness of the plan. Says the objector: You deliberately remove these complicated problems from familiar academic landmarks. You do not say how this general education is to be fused with the professional or vocational training that you regard as necessary or unavoidable. You do not say whether the study of personal relationships is to be a course or a curriculum. You propose to substitute for departmental organization, which is at least in being and familiar, some vague grouping of personnel into staff relationships. Are these units lecture courses, to be taught by sections or recitation affairs? Are you abolishing English composition as a universal requirement? In sum, are not your changes, however excellent in intent, dreamy and impractical in terms of the present American college?

I do not know the workable answer to every question of this order. It is, however, precisely because I do not know the answers to these pragmatical inquiries that I believe answers should be found. I must remind the reader again of Dean Carmichael's shrewd observation that we are carrying forward processes of education on essentially the same basis as that on which our predecessors dealt with them, notwithstanding the fact that the society into which graduates go has undergone marked change. It is not important how academic book-keeping readjusts itself to this six-point program; what is important is that the academic mind shall adjust itself to the atomic world. I hope it is not overly smug to observe that in setting forth educational aims thinkers from Plato to John Dewey have been as specific as they could be about the direction and purpose of education, leaving to others the implementation of their desires. The tentative program of this book is not, to put it mildly, of the order of Plato and Aristotle; it is something designed to get us through the next quarter of a century because the need for adjustment is urgent; but it is no more an objection to this program that it does not offer a blueprint of course credits, salaries, examinations, and other parts of the academic machine than it is an objection to *Emile* that Rousseau did not draw up a lawyer's contract for a teacher and a school. Administrators are quick at making adjustments when they see that adjustments have to be made; witness what they did to "normal" college work during the War.

III

The true weakness of what is here proposed is not to be discovered in the foregoing objections. Its true weakness, like the unconfessed weakness of schemes of general education now in operation or proposed, lies in the quality and training of those who are to teach. They are trained for years as specialists; yet they are expected to teach like philosophers. Naturally they do not succeed in teaching like philosophers, if they ever do, until after a painful and prolonged period of trial and error at the expense of the students. And when we ask where and when college teachers are trained, we must enter the portals of that mysterious institution, the graduate school of arts and sciences.

Some years ago President Isaiah Bowman of The Johns Hopkins University uttered a sentence which rings in my memory. Graduate education, he said, is the most expensive, the most important, and the least understood activity in American education. Nothing in the last half century alters the force of his terse statement. Graduate schools continue to flourish by educational neglect. Yet what is done today in the graduate schools directly or indirectly affects the colleges tomorrow and eventually, the rest of education. If you trace the stream of educational influence to its source, you will usually find it begins with the training of young doctors of philosophy in the graduate school.

The first, perhaps the last, fact about the graduate school of arts and sciences in any university is that it is usually a phantom. Its history makes it so. With three or four exceptions — Johns Hopkins, Chicago and Clark are such exceptions — the American graduate school developed as an extension of the American college and not as an educational entity in its own right. Typically, a four-year college under pressure to "offer more work" added a fifth year for an M.A. degree or (what amounts to the same thing) transformed an existing but empty M.A. into a degree resting upon course credits and not upon the mere payment of a fee. Eventually in one department and then in another, the college developed the Ph.D. Yet the chief labor of the faculty meanwhile is still undergraduate work, its budgetary support is based on the undergraduate curriculum, its effective head is dean of the undergraduate college, and the pressures upon it as a faculty from the alumni and the outside world are, so to speak, undergraduate pressures. In the last few years one has heard a great deal about the Harvard report, the Yale report or the Columbia program; reading these documents, one would never suspect that the Harvard graduate school, the Yale graduate school and the Columbia graduate school are in the long run far more powerful influences upon the current of American culture than are the undergraduate colleges concerning which these reports were made.

A graduate school of arts and sciences is theoretically a professional school having a professional aim. But its workings are strangely at variance with a unitary theory. To make this clear, consider the way any university president goes about constructing a new professional school other than the graduate school of arts and sciences. If he is putting together a medical school, its faculty will be chosen for the single purpose of concentrating upon medical education and research, independently of all other academic duties. An effective administrative head, the dean of the medical school, is placed in charge. Indeed, to discover such a person is well nigh the first duty of the founding university. An independent medical school budget is set up. The curriculum, determined by the medical faculty according to standards proposed by the profession, is established and has no other aim in view than maintaining or raising these standards. A constant interchange of ideas will go on between the new medical school and other medical schools as well as hospitals, organizations of doctors and surgeons, public health institutions, the army and navy and other appropriate bodies professionally concerned with medical care. Because medical education is under constant pressure to improve the quality of its graduates, students are selected with increasing rigor, methods of choice going back to the high school and qualities of personality being quite as basic in the selective process as academic or scholastic performance. Faults are alleged against medical

schools, but in comparison with the haphazard "selection" (or rather lack of selection) of students by
the graduate schools of arts and sciences, among them
candidates for the delicate art of teaching college
youth, medical education is a thousand miles nearer
perfection and illustrates the truth that professional
and vocational education in the United States makes
demands and secures results the colleges of liberal
arts cannot secure.

Similar programs are worked out *pari passu* in
other professional schools, such as those of law, engineering, commerce, public health or dentistry.
Meanwhile, however, almost anybody with a B.A.
from a relatively reputable institution can enter some
graduate school of arts and sciences, the baccalaure-
ate being the only *sine qua non* for entrance, and can
proceed to a degree which it requires a miracle of incompetence, if one judges by usual professional standards, to fail to take. Hence it is that the Ph.D.
finds few to praise it and very few to love. Yet so
conservative are most graduate deans that they are
unable or unwilling to admit that if methods of selecting students can be worked out successfully in the
case of college entrants, medical students, law students or engineers, the inference is irresistible that
methods of selection can be found for potential scholars and future professors, graduates of the graduate
schools of arts and sciences. So far, however, the

tentative Graduate Record Examination, almost literally forced upon the graduate schools by the Carnegie Foundation, is the sole contribution to selecting student personnel. and is even yet not universally required. If medical education had been thus backward, we should still be administering calomel.

In contrast to the unity of aim found in professional schools, the graduate school of arts and sciences possesses only a formal unity that does not integrate. Its faculty, as we have seen, is only the college faculty of arts and sciences in a partial capacity; its structure is so loose it can best be described as a congery of petty schools, one for each department offering advanced degrees, plus an indefinite number of "inter-departmental" programs; its administrative head, the graduate dean, in nine cases out of ten, does nothing in particular and doesn't even do that very well because he has only a shadowy clerical function and only illusory authority, principally as an unconfessed dean of students.[2] The budget for graduate instruction is commonly lost in the budgets of those more powerful units, the departments, so that it is difficult and usually impossible for a president to know what he pays for graduate work as distinguished from undergraduate instruction in the same

[2] In some institutions, however, as if further to increase national confusion in graduate education, the dean of the graduate school is vice-president of the university, one of the two or three most powerful personalities in the academic hierarchy. But this situation is atypical of the American university.

fields. There is seldom any agreement about the curricular needs of the school as a whole, new programs of
graduate instruction being added to a curriculum on
a system of polite academic horse-trading, whereby,
in return for voting for your pet program, I expect
you to vote for mine. No program is generally directed towards preparing young specialists for their
future common pedagogical and civic responsibilities.
Though students may work for either or both of two
degrees, the Association of American Universities in
all the years of its existence has never been able to
find out what the aim and content of an M.A. is supposed to be; and a doctor's degree in chemistry has
actually less relation to a doctor's degree in English
literature than it has to the "inferior" degree of B.A.
in Chemical Engineering. Such is the American graduate school.

All this is discouraging enough. There are yet
other baffling elements in graduate education. Graduate courses are usually taught by the oldest and
most conservative members of a given department,
men who, by reason of possessing indefinite tenure,
are or can be immune to educational change; and
since to them graduate work is a refuge from the in-
cessant and petty annoyances of the undergraduate
world, their attitude is, understandably, that this,
the holy of holies of pure scholarship and research
methodology, the sacred temple where the torch of

learning is handed on from generation to generation, shall not be laid hold of by profane hands. Consequently they silently resist attempts to orient or integrate graduate training along pedagogical lines because they are fearful that self-seeking administrators, shallow professors of education or other lesser breeds without the law shall sully the ark of the covenant.

And of course they are right if the sole responsibility of graduate education is to create an indefinite but increasing number of research workers. As this, though it is the theoretical aim of graduate training, is but the lesser part of the professional activities of a large proportion of its graduates; and as in fact the majority of graduate students and the majority of Ph.D.'s do not become research workers in any productive sense of the word except in a few departments of the school, the theoretical philosophy of graduate study and the actual *raison d'être* of most graduate students tend more and more to diverge, a tendency that increases in proportion as industry, government, libraries, research foundations and institutes of advanced study invade or take over research activities that were once the exclusive possession of the graduate school.

Specialism, sometimes rising little higher than specialized technology, is the primary aim and principle of organization in graduate education. But though I have remarked that the weakness of education at this level is that twenty-five departments of specialism will give you, not one, but twenty-five petty graduate schools, there is an interesting division even among these departments. In other professional schools the relation between training and actual professional practice is often close. For example, the Society for the Promotion of Engineering Education is an organization which has done useful work in checking over-theoretical developments in engineering education, by bringing the experience of employers to bear upon engineering colleges. In the graduate school of arts and sciences some areas of training have had the benefit of analogous practical criticism. The training of chemists, for example, has been greatly influenced by the expressed needs of industrial chemistry; and other sciences have had the benefit of similar experiences. In the social sciences economists may look forward to posts in government, commerce or international affairs no less than in teaching, and their training is naturally influenced by the fact that an agency outside the academic walls raises its powerful voice and speaks words of practical wisdom. Another channel for this influence is the in-training of lesser governmental officials in institutes of political science or the like, established in this or that university.

But the sole outlet for the humanities is, with rare exceptions, teaching; and from this patent fact two paradoxical results follow. The first is that since the sole criterion of success in the humanities is an academic criterion, academicism is not held in check as it is in chemistry or political science, but on the contrary is encouraged, the result being that theoretical demand can be piled upon theoretical demand without protest except from presidents and deans, until, as in the case of English studies, specialties multiply to a degree unparalleled in educational history. One man becomes expert in the bad — that is to say, the pirated — quartos of Shakespeare, but only for the seventeenth century; another devotes his energies, not to ballads, but to an index of the themes of ballads. Training of this kind and a professional aim of this order do not produce wise teachers; yet this training is stoutly defended in research circles as productive of that pure, though useless, scholarship society is mystically under obligation not merely to accept but also to support.

The second paradoxical result is that, although engineering schools, departments of chemistry or colleges of commerce pay some attention to the state of their labor market and try not to produce more technicians than industry, government and teaching can absorb (this attention, to be sure, is still imperfect and intermittent), those branches of learning which produce Ph.D.'s for college consumption only, make no effort to limit the number of candidates in terms of their probable success in finding jobs as teachers. Currently of course there is a bull market. Only a few years ago, however, a great department of history, after careful study, discovered it was creating more history teachers than the country needed, at least from this department. Ph.D.'s without jobs become embittered men. That the unemployed intellectual is a social menace the example of Europe shows us, but under the present philosophy scholarship is an absolute, to be pursued by as many persons possessing the minimum qualifications as choose to pursue it.

Such, then, are some of the baffling confusions of graduate education in American universities. In many ways this strange institution is more vividly and practically engaged with the problems of American society than is any other unit in our universities. Research in nuclear physics, the tax structure, adolescent psychology, growth hormones in plants, racial tension or the efficiency of congressional committees, initiated in the graduate school is direct, useful and influential. From astronomy at one end of the list of departments to zoology at the other there is no point at which the graduate faculty is not busily at work to supply our industrial culture with the expertized information it demands. The relevance of the information available in graduate work in the humanities and in history is somewhat less obvious than that offered by the sciences and the social sciences, but inasmuch as scholarship is usual in modern societies, charges of pedantry and antiquarianism, though they have, one fears, great force, may yet be discounted as coming from the philistine world. And yet, despite all this, one is struck by the patent truth that the graduate school of arts and sciences is curiously immunized against social currents and general ideas. It accepts no social responsibility as an educational institution. Its technological training for specialisms is superb; its general training almost non-existent. It makes no effort to instruct its students in a philosophy of life or of society or to train them for careers as college teachers or to prepare them broadly and generously and maturely to deal with the world. It will accept the neurotic personality as readily as it accepts any other kind, provided both have minimal ability; it will graduate them both and it will refuse to recognize any further obligation than to keep their records in an "appointment office" where they can be interviewed by deans and presidents, personnel directors or government chiefs looking for skilled technologists. One of the deepest needs in American education is to re-think the problem of the graduate school.

IV

The American graduate school of arts and sciences has not altered in essentials during the seventy or eighty years of its existence. Unless it alters, unless it can be made to face responsibility for general ideas and social aims no less than for technological training, current innovations in general education which arouse so much discussion in the public press remain little more than a new permutation of the same old elements. Yet the graduate school will not alter of its own volition, but only reluctantly and slowly in response to pressures. Whence are these pressures to come? Four possible sources occur to me.

The first source of pressure is from the schools and colleges of education which, having long dominated teacher training for the lower levels of education, have recently shown an increasing interest in the training of college professors and academic executives. In view of the failure of the graduate school to admit that the problem of training college teachers is anything more than teaching the candidate the rudiments of his specialty, this interest of the school or college of education is honorable, nor do I think so badly of professors of education as do most of my academic colleagues. But the hostility between the two faculties is great and traditional and seems, unfortunately, to increase as the place of teacher-training institutions in our society becomes more secure. It would be, I think, strategically unwise for the school of education at this juncture to try to force the graduate school to modernize its ways.

The second possibility is government pressure. We are entering an era in which governmental support of and interest in education, notably in the training of scientists, is steadily growing; and it is conceivable that federal grants to universities might be conditioned upon establishing the right kind of training for college professors. But the experience of state universities with legislative interference in academy policies has led their faculties to be suspicious of "political" controls; and federal pressures would do more harm than good.

A third possibility is the great educational foundations, such as the Rockefeller, the Carnegie and the Guggenheim. Progressive leaders of these influential corporations have long been disturbed by the failure of graduate schools to train the right sort of college teachers and by the failure to train the right sort the right way. These institutions are not suspected of wanting to "lower standards"; their interest in research is as keen as is the interest of the "graduate faculty"; they are not political bodies; they have both a national and an international interest; and they have great wealth. The creation of the Graduate Record Examination by the Carnegie Foundation shows that their contributions are not unacceptable to the graduate schools. Yet by themselves the foundations can do little more than study and advise. Joined with a fourth group, however, their aid may

prove crucial. Alone, they are helpless (except incidentally) to affect basic change.

The fourth source of pressure is the crucial source.
It is the principal employers of graduate students in
the world of arts and sciences — that is to say, the
liberal arts colleges themselves. Presidents and deans
of these institutions have for years inveighed against
the badness of doctoral training for their needs. Yet
they have continued for years abjectly to employ the
very Ph.D.'s they claim they do not want.

This curious professional cowardice (it deserves
the harsh noun) is understandable only as one realizes that in our competitive society the liberal arts
colleges fiercely battle with each other. This competition extends from scouting for future students in the
high schools to the thirst for proper "ratings" by various other educational units, for example, by law
schools admitting college students; and from solicit-
ing the great foundations for grants-in-aid to placat-
ing powerful alumni likely to leave bequests. Theirs
is a Darwinian world; theirs is the struggle to survive. Not to be properly "accredited," not to have
the right percentage of Ph.D.'s on the faculty, not to
play the game according to the rules but to play it
a little more skillfully and perhaps (dare one say
so?) a little more ruthlessly than one's competitor —
such has been the law of their being. Financial, intellectual and sociological pressures upon the colleges

have together discouraged educational independence.

Yet the presidents and deans of liberal arts colleges, to a degree they apparently do not suspect, hold in their hands the future of general education and of the right training of teachers in that area. Their present situation is something like that of the American high schools until recently. For years the American high schools stood in awe of the college, obediently offering "college entrance" subjects to pupils who had no intention of entering college. When they discovered that the meaning of secondary education was not bounded by the college entrance requirements and set up curricula for their own needs, they discovered also that the colleges were forced to give the high schools a high degree of autonomy and to accept as "college entrance" subjects what the high schools proposed to teach. The domination of the high schools by the colleges is not totally ended, the situation is not so simple as I have pictured it as being, right does not lie wholly with the high schools which, amidst many necessary changes, have also admitted much shoddy work, nor is the power of the colleges to insist upon certain topics being taught to applicants for admission ended. Nevertheless, it is the high schools which now lead and the colleges which now follow.

The colleges are organized into professional associations such as the Association of American Colleges.

On the parallel of the influence emanating from the Society for the Promotion of Engineering Education, such an organization could, if it so desired (and why should it not?), declare in forthright terms what kind of product they desire from the graduate schools. They could (and ought) to work out positive programs of training, or if not that, at least positive aims for such training, set forth in good round terms. They ought likewise to indicate to the graduate schools not merely the dissatisfactions they have with the present Ph.D. program, but the specific instances and causes of that dissatisfaction. They ought, furthermore, flatly to refuse to hire Ph.D.'s trained the wrong way. The colleges are now of age; however useful for raising standards it may once have been to count faculty degrees as an accrediting device, the time is long past when this simple mechanical performance has meaning — if for no other reason, then for the reason that the Ph.D., according to the colleges themselves, has become mediocre. The colleges are in a unique position to speak boldly to the graduate schools. If they would do so, the picture of training for college professors would alter for the better in short order.

It is furthermore conceivable, in view of associations like that in engineering, in view of the dissatisfactions expressed by Dean Donham of the Business School, and in view of the uneasiness of other vocational and technical associations regarding the too narrow range of interests among graduates entering this or that special field, that any positive and forthright demand made by the colleges would receive unexpected support.

But pressure upon graduate education must be wisely exerted. We cannot, even if we wanted to, prevent graduate schools from being what they are supposed to be; namely, institutions for specialists. The colleges, furthermore, fall into serious error if they ignore the patent truth that they, too, are engaged in professional or vocational training. A technological society is going to have its experts, and graduate schools exist to produce their share of specialists. The problem cannot be solved in terms of vague good will. What practical alterations are possible?

THE PLACE OF UNDERSTANDING

V

THE PLACE OF UNDERSTANDING

Our exploration of the relation between education and world tragedy opened with a picture of the last half century — fifty years dominated by war and slaughter, moral disintegration and physical destruction. Modern warfare, however, is impossible without the technical training needed to produce its weapons and to direct its dreadful course; and this technical education originates in the colleges and universities, in which preparation for war and the business of war itself are increasingly influential elements, so much so that in time of armed conflict higher education becomes a branch of the armed services. In addition, an unacknowledged chauvinism, itself the cause and consequence of war, complicates the educational problem by confusing cosmopolitan and international culture with national ideology. One World cannot merely image the United States.

Because higher education is theoretically one of the guides in any modern culture, the tragic failure of western civilization has led to a series of educational changes at the college level, mainly originating in non-scientific portions of the faculty. Some wish to impose a dogmatic unity upon the college; others de-

sire to retire upon western tradition. Neither dog-
matist nor traditionalist faces such crucial issues as
the fact that, acknowledge it or not, the liberal arts
college devotes most of its energies to one or another
program of professional or vocational training or that
the reaffirmation of "western tradition" in a world
led to destruction by men in that tradition is poor
preparation for One World.

There is need in education for a philosophy which,
if the United States is to survive, must spring from a
democratic dynamic not yet formulated. Pending its
creation and as a step towards that creation, it is here
urged that, at least for one or two decades, our tragic
need will be best met by recognizing that young persons launching into competitive society must be vo-
cationally or professionally trained if they are to survive, and that in the long run the acceptance by the
colleges of this stubborn fact will do more for "general education" than a genteel denial of its existence.
Pending the creation of a dynamic for democratic
culture not merely nationalistic in aim, education
ought to include the study of scientific method and
the results of the application of science to industrial
society; representative government; the cultures of
Russia and the Orient; and the question of personal
relationships in a world where insecurity steadily
weakens man's trust in his fellow man. But neither
this temporary program nor any other program of

"general education" can in the long run avoid degenerating into the particularism (that bane of departmentalized education) unless properly trained teachers can be found. The present American graduate school offers small possibility for creating such a teaching personnel. Its business is with specialisms. Such has been the line of our argument. What changes are possible in graduate education?

Despite the wild illogicalities of their make-up, existing graduate schools of arts and sciences perform too useful a function and are too deeply imbedded in university structure for any immediate alteration. If they change, they will change with glacial slowness. Our culture is highly technical; and precisely as medical schools, dental schools, engineering schools and the like maintain our superb technology by raising up new generations of experts, so graduate schools will continue to produce the chemists, biologists, physicists, mathematicians and other scientists we need, not to speak of economists, anthropologists and historians. Whether literary scholars, philosophers and linguists are not in fact also technologists of books is a point much debated. The rigidity of most "humanistic" writing creates no great belief that literary studies arising from research training differ in quality from that of other technical specialties.

The fact that liberal arts colleges are in truth institutions giving professional or vocational training means that large sections of their faculties will be recruited from the existing graduate schools. The beginning biologist *qua* biologist must be trained by experts in biology, not by sentimental reformers; and no amount of sociological disquisition about the effects of science on manufacture will ground the beginner in the elementary knowledge basic to the work of a future industrial chemist. Indeed, franker recognition by presidents and deans of these colleges, of the dual nature of their work, by clarifying the status and function of experts as over against courses in general education, ought not merely to improve college faculties by defining more clearly the proper business of the specialist, it ought also to aid the graduate school. This institution is not equipped for philosophic breadth, but for specialization.

Moreover, to expect existing graduate schools to produce proper teachers of general education is to add a fourth and impossible burden to an already bewildered faculty. It will be recalled that in nine institutions out of ten, the faculty of the graduate school of arts and sciences is in fact merely the faculty of the college seen in a partial aspect. At the present time in any typical American university the same group of human beings are trying simultaneously to perform three heavy and inharmonious tasks. They are, in one part of the college day, trying to give "general education" to undergraduates, most of whom are vague as to what they are doing because the college elaborately pretends that students are not to be concerned with earning a living. In another part of the college day (sometimes to the same classes) they are trying to give expert professional or vocational training at more or less elementary levels to both undergraduates and graduates. In a third portion of their time (and perhaps again to the same classes) they are, as members of the graduate faculty, trying to give the most expert training possible to candidates for the most advanced degrees offered by the institution. To expect that these same men shall take on yet a fourth task — the task of producing college professors rather than expert research workers — is to expect the impossible. Those portions of such a faculty whose primary business is with purely academic matters like English literature and the other humanities are, of course, somewhat more aware of the problem of educating college professors than is, to choose an example at random, a department of chemistry, most of whose graduate students enter the industrial field, but it is nonetheless broadly true that the faculty of arts and sciences, already suffering confusion of aims resulting from incompatible demands cannot end the confusion by fulfilling more demands.

One can only wish, as I do, that the graduate school were other than it is. Its lack of social responsibility, its failure to inculcate philosophical breadth, its refusal to select its students wisely, its content with specialisms foster the technological difficulties of our culture. Indeed, such stray members of any "graduate faculty" as express an active interest in politics, sociology or government in the sense of a real concern for the nation and the world are normally regarded by their colleagues as having betrayed the pure research spirit or having failed as investigators of their specialties. The "graduate faculty" tacitly expects to be supported by society in the interests of pure learning; it does not recognize its own reciprocal social obligations. But although I believe these comments to be just, although I believe there is a working relation between modern warfare, technology, technological education and nationalism on the one side and the socially irresponsible research spirit of the graduate schools on the other, we cannot get along without research and we cannot get along without graduate education.

I suggest therefore that since we cannot hope to remake these powerful institutions with their great virtues and their great defects, we retain them. But let us give such a school a name which designates its real function. Let us call it the Research Training Institute. Its sole purpose shall be the creation of research workers for the academic world and for the worlds of business, industry and government. Its sole degree shall be the Ph.D., inasmuch as the amorphous M.A.

is an acknowledged failure as a research degree. Let us, if we can, improve the organization of such a Research Training Institute by strengthening the power of its dean and giving it a greater degree of autonomy than the present graduate school possesses. If we cannot set up a separate faculty for it (and it is unlikely that we can), let us at least, by insisting that its sole business is the training of research workers, so far simplify the labors of the faculty of arts and sciences as to consolidate their obligations as a graduate faculty. As the faculty of the Research Training Institute, their business will be to select and train research workers — that is, specialists in the various departments of knowledge. This will free professors from the duty of doing two incompatible things at once — training mature students for research and at the same time laying the basis of a broad, general or philosophical education. I do not regard this change, I repeat, as ideal, but I think it is the only practical move in our present situation.

But where and how are college professors competent to carry on the general work of the liberal colleges to be trained?

II

I believe we must create in selected universities hospitable to the idea a new graduate educational unit to be called the Graduate College, the primary purpose of which shall be not the training of research workers but the education of persons competent to teach intelligently the general work of the liberal college. I refer, of course, not to experts trained in the Research Training Institute and in charge of professional or vocational training programs which the college must retain, but to broadly educated men and women able to administer general education maturely, richly and with a high sense of its import. That is, they will want to make a career of it and not take it on as an extra burden.

Parenthetically, their relation in the college faculty to the departments, which are, as it were, the research experts, will have to be patterned upon the relation of the humanistic (non-scientific) faculty of a technological institute to its specialized programs and professional departments. That relation, it is true, is everywhere unsatisfactory, one cause of dissatisfaction being the bad training of humanists for posts that require notable maturity. Nevertheless, here is the nearest working equivalent to an actual but unacknowledged division of functions in existing college faculties. The amalgamation of the work of departments giving professional or vocational training with this general education should begin in the freshman year and be continuous throughout college, as I have earlier indicated, a problem of administration that will require great tact and skill. Nevertheless, college education should be a natural growth, not progress through a layer cake. But the administrative problem, though complex, is not here our concern. How shall the Graduate College, intended for the education of such persons, be constituted? How shall it go to work?

In the first place, the Graduate College must be a small but completely autonomous unit, having its own head, its own budget, its own faculty, its own curriculum and its own quarters. Nothing less will do. It must be empowered to send its students into other parts of the university, as we shall see, but it must remain distinct in structure and spirit from the Research Training Institute, from the general undergraduate-graduate faculty of arts and sciences, and from the other professional and vocational schools and colleges constituting the university. It must grant its own degrees, select its own students, and offer its own fellowships and scholarships. And it must maintain its own professional liaison with such organizations as the Association of American Colleges, a relation analogous in part to that of the engineering schools to the Society for the Promotion of Engineering Education.

A faculty of from seven to twelve should suffice. This faculty should be full professors, or at the utmost, full professors and associate professors, in order that the bickerings of academic preferment and the jockeying for appointment may be reduced. They should not be organized into departments, though their numbers should as a matter of course include representatives of all the parts of learning, broadly considered — the humanities, the social sciences, and science itself. But it should not include linguists *qua* linguists, economists who have just invented a new system or zoologists who are famous for rarefied research work. Persons of this calibre belong in the faculty of the Research Training Institute. The faculty of the Graduate College should consist of persons whose professional history perhaps began with research work but who have since come to reflect philosophically upon science, the arts and the social sciences in relation to human culture, notably in relation to education as a social and intellectual process. In sum, the spirit in which this faculty is to be appointed is the spirit in which a "university professor" is occasionally appointed now. Such an appointment usually connotes intellectual maturity and philosophic growth which has passed beyond (peace to specialists!) mere research. This obvious requirement is a second reason for admitting to the faculty of the Graduate College only persons worth at least an associate professorship.

The selection and appointment of such a faculty will be of course a difficult task. How far a "dean" is necessary for so small a group remains to be seen. My

own feeling is that a group of this sort does not require anything more than a chairman; that, although
in the first instance the creation of such a faculty
should require the utmost wisdom in the appointing
officers of a university, the group itself should thereafter recommend new appointments to the president
of the university; and that administrative machinery
need not go much beyond an office of records. The
principal difficulty will be the selection of students.

The number of students admitted to study in the
Graduate College should be small. The utmost number at any time should be a hundred; I should myself
prefer sixty or seventy-five. Fifty would be better
still. And this number should be selected by the faculty of the Graduate College itself, and the faculty
should be the sole agent in this selective process. I
lay some stress upon this obvious requirement because of the variety of ways students now enter existing graduate schools.

The avowed aim of the Graduate College being the
creation of professors for the liberal college (rather
than expert research workers who belong in the Research Training Institute), the first criterion in the
selection of students for this college must be the gen-
uineness of their own interest in teaching at the college level as a career. The Graduate College cannot
admit to its curriculum graduate students cynically
"going after" a Ph.D. because they need the union

label. On the contrary, the entire spirit of the student body like that of its faculty must perpetually battle against this mechanical interpretation of advanced study. Admission to the Graduate College must therefore depend upon a series of tests and interviews at least as rigorous as those which now admit to the medical school, the law school or the business school, though the tests to be devised must of course be relevant to the business of the Graduate College. From the beginning, in other words, the Graduate College ought to be difficult to get into. In no other way can its appeal be genuine. The selective process should resemble that of the Guggenheim Fellowships or that of admission to the Institute of Advanced Study or any other intellectual recognition of outstanding merit. To be known as a student of the Graduate College in such and such a university ought, in sum, to carry with it *réclame* comparable in kind to being awarded a Rockefeller Grant, winning a Harvard Sheldon Fellowship or being appointed a Rhodes Scholar. The Graduate College is neither just another graduate school nor a glorified teachers college.

So far as course instruction in the Graduate College is concerned, it should be kept as informal as possible. The discussion group, the friendly give-and-take seminar rather than the seminar of formal paper and

dreary report, directed readings, personal conferences
— these rather than lecture courses or other conventional classroom activities should be the spirit of the
enterprise. The Graduate College is not a place to
learn foreign languages, master the rudiments of
mathematics, be introduced to beginning biology or
read for the first term a text in economics or history.
It should be a place to reflect upon and to discuss the
philosophy of language and the meaning of literature,
the social, metaphysical and pedagogical problems
arising from mathematics, theories of science and
their application, and the uses of history and the
other social sciences for modern man. The discussion
of these and similar problems should be guided by
those members of the faculty of the Graduate College
best informed and most interested in the sector of
learning concerned. But the philosopher should not
be prevented from discussing science and history, the
economist and the scientist from disputing the philosopher or the poet from challenging the assumptions
of the scientist, all in the interest of achieving an educational affirmation proper to democratic society.

The work of students in the Graduate College need
not be confined, however, to instruction in that College. The faculty of the Graduate College should be
empowered to send its students anywhere in the university (or, for that matter, outside it) as their edu-

cational needs require. I have in mind the excellent formula for the Nieman Fellowships in Journalism at Harvard University. The holder of such a fellowship may attend any class in any part of Harvard University; he does not have to enroll in a particular school or college, embark upon its degree program and so cut himself off from the rest of the university. He enjoys, in other words, the prerogative which any mature student should have but which our existing schemes of graduate education have mostly ended.

So the student in the Graduate College desiring to become a teacher of science and of the meaning of science in the sense that general education programs have in mind, ought to be empowered by the Graduate College to attend such courses in biology, chemistry, physics, geology or the like as his professional preparation and his interests may require. But he need not necessarily enroll in research courses. He does not have to follow some research program in nuclear physics in the Research Training Institute. He desires, in sum, to secure knowledge and the "feel" of materials; he does not need to become a technologist. He needs to bring to the discussion of science and the scientific method in the Graduate College informed and, in a reasonable sense of the word, expert opinion, and to that end he ought to do some laboratory work and sit in some advanced courses in science in the university, but he ought not to be trained for research activities. And what is true of the candidate in science should be equally true of the candidate in the social sciences or in the arts.

This relation will of course be difficult to work out. The professional scholar or the expert scientist is likely to infer that the student from the Graduate College is another annoying dilettante. If he wants to learn biology, why doesn't he take the research degree? And the expert, having had some experience with other candidates (for example, those in education) who have perhaps tried to avoid the rigors of laboratory technique and whose intellectual equipment was not overwhelming will have to be persuaded that the student from the Graduate College is not of this calibre. Only two facts can so persuade him. One is his respect for that member of the Graduate College who sent the student to the expert. The other is the intellectual ability of the student himself. Both are problems of choice. Both illustrate the necessity for the most careful selection of faculty and student body for the Graduate College.

A third element in Graduate College training is implicit in the discussion. We have spoken of work in the Graduate College itself and of sending the student into courses offered elsewhere in the university. The first is intended to educe philosophical consideration of the problems of the fields of knowledge; the second, to assure a sufficient degree of expert awareness. But the candidate is to become a college professor competent to teach programs of general education. He must therefore be led to reflect upon the nature of college education and of its meaning for the world. Some discussion of the philosophy of education, of the nature of culture and of the relation of American civilization to the rest of the world is central to this program. It may therefore be thought that a professor of the philosophy of education should be appointed to the Graduate College. That in particular instances such an appointment can be made follows from the general theory of this faculty, which is to be representative rather than departmental. But it does not follow that a professor of the philosophy of education is a *sine qua non*. Rather these questions should be the central and common concern of the entire faculty of the Graduate College, the one "requirement" around which all else revolves. And the problem of any possible training for classroom teaching is a problem to be solved by the whole faculty, not by an "expert" in education. It may be that in his final year the candidate should teach, proper arrangements having been made in some college of the university or elsewhere. It may be that the candidates should teach each other in small classes. It may be that a seminar in the history of collegiate education is desirable. The important thing, however, is not *falsely to expertize* college education, but to make this professional end the responsibility of students and faculty alike.

What degree should the Graduate College award? However its work may differ in kind from that of the Research Training Institute, it will fail if its training does not equal it in depth and rigor. A three-year graduate curriculum should therefore lead to the Ph.D. degree. I have at various times thought that it might be possible to rehabilitate the M.A. degree as a mark of proper training for general work of this order; I conclude for practical reasons that this is impossible. Unless some other degree can be invented, the Graduate College should therefore administer a doctoral program as rigorous as any other. If a special designation is needed, let the candidate be awarded a Ph.D. in the Arts, in the Social Sciences, or in Science.

Should a dissertation be required? A research dissertation in the usual sense is alien to the spirit of the Graduate College. But that its candidates should be required to display intellectual maturity by the independent treatment of important issues of interpretation, whether the material is new and unique or not, seems patent. Whether, however, a dissertation is the proper mode for this evidence may be debated. Others may incline to a series of mature essays in the second or third year of the candidate's career, mounting perhaps into some sort of personal and professional unity. Matters of this order are for the faculty of the Graduate College to determine, it being constantly kept in mind that the intellectual demands upon the candidates shall be at least as severe as and, if possible, should surpass those upon graduates of the Research Training Institute. So, too, in the matter of examinations for the degree. The rote examination too common in graduate schools tests little except the memory of the candidate and the patience of the committee in charge. But that candidates should be under constant scrutiny by the faculty, that the faculty should be ruthless in weeding out incompetent material, if such slips by the selective process, that the Graduate College diploma should be the seal of approval placed upon candidates of great promise, fine personality, richness of background and zeal for collegiate education — all this is, though elementary, to be kept constantly in mind. General graduate education will not profit by anything short of the highest standards of maturity. The fact that a given candidate means well or has tried hard or has an ailing mother or needs a job — excuses for awarding current graduate degrees — has no place in the Graduate College.

Two elements of present graduate student life, however, require change. In the present graduate world, life is too close to the economic ragged edge. Candidates for the highest degree in the gift of American universities are permitted by these same universities to live in wretched rooms, to eat poor food, to exist without recreation and to envy the sheltered dormitory life of undergraduates, housing whom is too frequently a political matter agreeable to alumni interests or to self-seeking state officials. Indeed, nothing is more curious in American education than that the most expensive products of the university system are treated, so far as their social existence is concerned, with general neglect. Freshmen are housed, disciplined, watched over; special officials are appointed to guide their faltering feet; if the university cannot house all its students, it is sure to house its freshmen, or at least as many of them as it can; and on the moral, social and intellectual well-being of immature high school graduates is lavished an amount of time, energy and attention beyond the dreams of the graduate school. But if, as President Bowman says, graduate education is the most important, the most expensive and the least understood activity in American education, surely its importance and its cost merit a far larger share of the social program of any university than it customarily receives.

All graduate students should be housed and fed by universities in a manner at least equal to that of undergraduates. The ordinary facilities of medical care, recreation, social life and the like services within the university should be available to them as, in too many cases, they are not now available. But what is generally true of all graduate students is especially true for students in the Graduate College, since upon their skill in social adjustment, their experience in social living, and their capacity to mediate among specialists depends the success of any college program of general education.

I should therefore make the creation of a residence building for students in the Graduate College a prerequisite to the existence of such a school. Such a residence unit should be of the character of the Harvard houses or the Yale colleges. One or other of the faculty of the Graduate College should be a resident in the house — the master of it, in Harvard or Yale phraseology. The house should have suitable bedrooms for students, suitable dining rooms, suitable recreation rooms, and small, informal rooms for seminars, meetings and the like activities of the school. A library should contain books for recreational reading and serve also for general meetings to be addressed by visitors as well as for dances and other social gatherings. In sum, both for its own sake and for the sake of preparing its students to live in the American college, the graduate program here sketched must be so housed as to insure gracious living.

But the facilities of such a housing unit will cost money, the tuition rate, together with the expenses of house living, is likely to be more than the pocketbook of most graduate students can afford, and unless the university establishing such a unit is prepared to create and maintain a foundation for the support of the Graduate College, grant a wide variety of fellowship aids, and squarely face the problem of the cost of graduate education, nothing of this program is possible in the right terms. A timid approach is worse than none. The issue is clear: either the education of college teachers in a world tragically in need of unity is worth all it costs or may cost, or it is not. One cannot prove that existing methods of graduate education are wasteful, and so far as the creation of technologists and research workers is concerned, they are perhaps not too inefficient. That, however, our present rule-of-thumb, hit-and-miss, laissez-faire modes of admitting students to graduate education must be wasteful seems *à priori* true, and certainly as a mode for selecting and training teachers of general education for college youth, present methods and present degrees seems to some of us indefensible. A Graduate College may initially prove to be a costly entity; but in the long run it will prove to be the least costly, the most important and the best understood program for creating and maintaining college professors to whom general training shall be both a passion and a career.

III

Only through exposing the future college professor to the play of general ideas, only by attempting to acquaint him with the social, political and intellectual responsibilities of One World, only by demanding that he be trained philosophically and not technically alone, can our colleges hope to restrain the professional and vocational demands made upon them, within proper bounds and to counteract the specialisms of the departments. We cannot, bad as they are, abolish departments; we cannot, despite the well-rounded periods of educational reformers, alter the fact that students go to college in order to equip themselves for a competitive society. Our only hope is not to abolish or ignore professional or vocational training, but to recognize it for what it is, and to raise programs of general education to an intellectual dignity and an immediacy of meaning equal to that of the professional or vocational curriculum. Such a program of general education, as I have indicated, has got to face and penetrate our tragic world, not flee from it into an agreeable past. But such a program must also be officered by teachers of the highest intelligence and tact, if it is to be successfully amalgamated with a proper and understandable desire upon the part of young America to be equipped for jobs. I suggest therefore the creation of the Graduate College as the means of creating such teachers. Except in rare instances I do not see how they can come out of existing graduate schools.

Of course a thousand difficulties immediately arise. The nature of the two functions — professional or vocational training and general education on one level, the work of the Research Training Institute and that of the Graduate College on another level — can never be sharply differentiated. Both the program proposed in general education and the creation of a Graduate College in some sense threaten the traditional prerogatives of the departmental system. Deans, chairmen and professors resist change. Budgetary difficulties of great magnitude and complexity arise. It will be argued that the reforms proposed lower standards or fail to meet the very issues, the discussion of which has led to the suggested reform. It will be said there will be no market for holders of degrees from the Graduate College. It will be argued that the more numerous products of the Research Training Institute will outweigh and outvote the slighter contingent in general education. It will be asked, who has the courage to bell the cat? In sum, all the traditional arguments of conservatism, wittily summarized in Sydney Smith's parody, "Noodle's Oration," can be brought to bear against change.

But could we in our wildest moments invent graduate education for ordinary college teachers more inappropriate than that they now receive? It is universally admitted that the majority of the students in our existing graduate schools will never become research workers in any real sense; yet, because there is nowhere else for them to go, they must go into graduate schools. The only formal training available for somebody who wants to teach in college is training for activity he will not carry on, or carry on only intermittently, casually, and with a cynical eye for promotion. Presidents and deans are overwhelmingly of the opinion that existing doctoral programs do not produce the kind of men they want; yet they seem utterly helpless to suggest change. Surely it is not unreasonable to suggest the time has come for differentiation of function at the graduate level.

Our situation resembles, it seems to me, that which obtained when The Johns Hopkins University opened its doors in 1876. A pessimist then viewing the vast disorganization of American academic education might reasonably have said of the little enterprise in Baltimore that it was a hare-brained attempt. You cannot, he would have argued, reverse the stream of education by calling upon a few men to set their faces against the current. Nevertheless, the Baltimore group was right and the pessimist would have been wrong. The creation of a modern research university in Maryland proved to be a catalytic agent, its influence was quickly and widely felt, and within twenty-five years the face of university education had changed.

There are times when the climate of opinion is favorable to pedagogical revolution. In higher education it would seem that the time is now.

There are at least two areas in the country favorable to this change. One is the eastern seaboard with its great private universities, many of them already committed to one or another program in general education. Nearer the great foundations, nearer also in some sense to the headquarters of influential educational groups and desirous of equalling and, if possible, surpassing the state universities, these institutions are in an excellent position to experiment in graduate education. The nature of the Graduate College herein outlined is based in part on academic reforms at the undergraduate level already undertaken in these schools. Their budgets are more flexible, and they have more immediate appeal to a loyal and wealthy alumni. Here is one promising area.

The second is in the South, never more alert to issues in graduate education than at the present time. Until the creation of the New England Conference on Graduate Education two or three years ago, the only professional body in the country directly concerned with graduate education and with nothing else was the Association of Southern Graduate Deans. The quiet, unpublicized meetings of this group have already done much for professional training in that vast region.

Moreover, the South is freer from the dead weight of tradition than are some other areas of the country. Its graduate education has not yet hardened. Its industrial and agricultural development is making new demands upon schools and colleges; and the growth of Southern liberal arts colleges is steady. The South looks back with pride upon a tradition in education that began with a pedagogical revolution. That tradition goes back at least to the revolutionary Thomas Jefferson, to whom, it is interesting to note, all schools of academic reform now appeal.

I do not recall that Jefferson himself was the product of a graduate school but I do recall that he united harmoniously vocational skill and general training. It is, indeed, an ironical comment upon the conventional Ph.D. that the only doctorates awarded to Washington, Madison, Monroe, John Taylor of Caroline or others like them, if they had any at all, were honorary degrees. All this suggests that education in the South, though often conservative, is not yet codified. It suggests that the South might want to create a Research Training Institute for one sort of proficiency and a Graduate College for another. If the South has been favored in the creation by private wealth of Duke University or in the rapid growth at public expense of an institution like the University of North Carolina, a pioneer in a dozen fields, it is not impossible to surmise that the South may see its present opportunity in graduate education.

But if neither the South, the East nor any other part of the country rises to the challenge of our time, what is the alternative except to continue the dizzy spiral of a higher and higher degree of specialization in the graduate world, a less and less degree of relevance of graduate training to that general education we all desiderate, a greater and greater confusion as to the place and purpose of the college in American society? Merely to insist upon the mystical priority of knowledge for its own sake, training for its own sake and graduate degrees for their own sake, especially in view of the growing cynicism about the Ph.D., is simply to intensify the bent of Americans toward the highest technological culture and the most inefficient social engineering in the world. We cannot by the mere accumulation of specialists, however brilliant, pass to general views. We cannot at one and the same time educate the young through specialists who know their trades and professions, and also through well-meaning, but vague, genteel professors, teaching general courses. We cannot hire Peter and be surprised because he is not Paul. The paramount need in the American academic world is for social vision; except in rare instances social vision does not come from the angle of present graduate education. How shall we secure social vision if we do not insist on training likely to create it?

IV

The immediate future of the United States will lie
to a degree unprecedented in the after-history of any
other war in the hands of the eleven million veterans
who fought World War II or who maintained the
fighting forces. At the moment they are flooding the
colleges. Their influence, their wants, their aims will
be decisive. I have asked an intelligent and sensitive
graduate student who served in the navy during the
war what his generation wants of education and of
American democracy. His report is literally this:

"The question of what the returning veterans want
can be answered only by reference to the fact that the
war generations have known two major influences on
their lives. The second was of course their experience
in World War II, but the first is equally important. It
is the Great Thirties Depression, during which these
men spent at least their boyhood, if not their youth
and young manhood. It was the bitterness and grey
desolation of so much of life in this century's fourth
decade which produced the soldiers of the war years,
men who fought bravely with little faith, whose most
immediate social reaction was distrust, whose dominant intellectual temper and defense was irony.

"The War, however, provided for these soldiers, as
for the rest of their country, the emotional dynamic
of a common purpose, the defense of the homeland at
first, and later, the destruction of those nations which

had produced the terrible menace. It was a job to be done, one of such obvious importance that in the doing of it one could endure, with the usual military griping, the great perils and hardships involved, to say nothing of the undemocratic inequities of the military caste system. With the end of the War this consuming emotional impetus was removed, and with it went the inarticulate sense of unity which the common purpose and the enforced necessity of working together had generated. The veterans ached to be free of military caste and to return to a type of life where the danger of sudden, violent death seemed less common; but at the same time they realized that they must now reintegrate themselves with the society which had produced the Great Depression, a society which placed its premium on selfishness and greed and which nevertheless could give no sure promise that the cycle of boom and bust would not be repeated. Throughout the war years a standing joke had been, "And where are you going to have *your* apple stand?" It was as though they were fighting to make the world safe for unemployment.

"So the returning veterans look first for financial security in an economic society, concerning which they are cynical whether they accept the system (as they usually do) or not. Their second desire is for a satisfactory resolution of sexual needs. Most seem to hope for a resolution which will offer as much sta-

bility and permanence as is possible in human relationships. They became increasingly convinced during the War that sex and morals are not necessarily
connected, but now they wish to find sexual relationships which will give them, as with a safe job, a sense
of security, dependability and trust. Once these two
major desires are satisfied, they can indulge their
third desire, which is simply to enjoy life.

"Veterans are convinced that the most generous
opportunity offered by the country in recognition of
their wartime service is that for education. They are
almost universally serious in their approach to these
educational opportunities. They attend classes regularly and on time, and cause discipline problems less
frequently than the usual high school or college students. This is the result not of habituation to military
discipline, but rather of the veterans' own decision.
They are convinced with a certainty lacking in the
average non-veteran student that they want education and want all they can get.

"Why do they want education? Some of those
whose education was interrupted by their entrance
into the armed forces may feel that they have missed
those nameless and vague 'opportunities,' that standard and vague argument in support of American education, and some may consider the exploitation of
their claims on the federal government for education
as a pleasant temporary delay to the necessity of

making their livings completely by themselves; yet the proved seriousness of most veterans in high school and college indicates that these two groups are small in number. An additional percentage feel that in 'education' they can find the answers to philosophical or socio-economic questions which troubled them in the depression and war years, can find the reasons behind the horrible waste of natural resources and human lives, those wealths of nations; but the American mind is primarily empirical, and the number of veterans who now pursue knowledge *qua* knowledge is again probably small.

"What most veterans want from education is the acquisition of technical and professional skills in order to increase their chances for reinstating themselves in our unsympathetic economic society. They know that education correlates with job possibilities, having seen that the amount of formal education frequently meant the difference between being an officer and being an enlisted man. They know that on the whole the trained man is the first to get a job, the most likely to get a well-paid job — and the one who has the best chance of survival when the bottom drops out of the boom. In the fight for survival, education gives him weapons against his fellows. It is not his fault that he thinks of contemporary American civilization in such terms; it is the fault of civilization itself, which promised housing for veterans and their families and can scarcely provide enough slums, which promised a higher standard of living and provides, instead, a higher cost of it, which promised freedom from fear and want, and seems intent on providing freedom for fear and want. To the veterans training in a skill or a profession feels like the weight of a good rifle in the hand."

This is a sobering statement, which should be pondered by college professors and administrators who think the remedy for our ills is "humanism." It is, of course, one man's statement, and others may bring in a differing report. But it is a statement expressive of a common attitude, one that must be reckoned with. It illuminates with a sudden piercing light the need for a democratic dynamic in our sick society. If general education, liberal education, college education — call it what you will — is to furnish its share of that cultural dynamic, it must face the fact that men want training in order to survive in a competitive civilization. If education is in any way to counteract the crudities of this drive for training, it must focus its attention upon the world as it is, not the world as it has been. If education is to prevent or check the corrosion eating into western culture, it must pass beyond western culture to view dispassionately and to consider the fate of mankind as a whole, over the surface of the entire globe. If education is to be effective in this respect, its teachers must be trained for that purpose, not for an opposite and contradictory one.

To begin, as this book has done, with compiling statistics about the slaughter of the last fifty years and to end with a plea for re-thinking the problem of graduate training may well seem a ridiculous and mouselike anti-climax. I have said that the contribution of formal education to solving the riddle of our world can be but small. It is the dark heart of man that is at fault, not the dim cloisters of our gothic universities. And yet we also began by pointing out how the technological spirit has seized upon educational processes once supposed to be philosophical. Ours is an engineering age. The trouble is that we have brought the engineering solution into college education and then wonder why we have no philosophy. Even our teachers of literature are specialists.

The values that may help our sick society will come, not from the dictates of specialism, but only as we have the courage in our colleges, so far as they can help, to face directly the tragic dilemma of our era. This must be the center of our general studies. That dilemma is a dilemma of thought and culture, not a dilemma of technique. Its history is important only in that small degree that historical considerations can help us to a present cure, and that degree (peace to academic specialists) is very small, indeed. The kingdom of the specialist is not the world of humanity.

Convinced, then, that pure specialism cannot in itself help us to solve our principal problem, I have therefore argued that the root of our educational difficulty goes back to the graduate schools. The problem of graduate training, too little known, too little studied, too superficially dealt with, too potent in its final effects upon world culture to be left to technologists and specialists, must be studied by thoughtful Americans. If the improvements suggested here do not please, then other changes must be found. We cannot go on by merely intensifying technological skills. For, as the late President Roosevelt said:

The mere conquest of our enemy is not enough. To-day we are all faced with the pre-eminent fact that if civilization is to survive we must cultivate the science of human relationships, the ability of *all* kinds to live together and work together in the same world at peace.